Echols From The Grave

By

Alicia Ford

Echols From The Grave
ISBN 978-1-7373694-9-3 Softbound
ISBN 979-8-9859076-0-5 Hardbound
ISBN 979-8-9859076-2-9 EBook
Copyright © 2022 Alicia Ford

Request for information should be addressed to:
Curry Brothers Marketing and Publishing Group
P.O. Box 247 Haymarket, VA 20168

Executive Editing by Jacqueline Lemus
Cover Design by Alex Cotton *(Unrelenting Media)*
Manuscript Formatting Copy Edit by Angel Ford

CURRY BROS.
MARKETING + PUBLISHING GROUP

Table of Contents

Dedication

I would like to dedicate this book to all the beautiful souls whom I have had the pleasure to come across and the not-so-beautiful souls. To me, everybody has a soul worth saving.

To My Beloved Husband, and our Seven Blessings from heaven and their Good Fruit.

My family by DNA and my family in Spirit and in Truth, my New family (I am so happy to have met you and look forward to getting to know you!).

To all who dare to resolve their hurt, shame, brokenness by facing it with zeal. To those who have made the commitment to life and devotion of faithfulness by undertaking the challenges of love and hope and for their prayers to be answered.

Echols Family Cemetery
Texas, USA

Preamble

Echols From The Grave

It has been said, "Life is full of surprises." What is not as often said is that those surprises may be good or not so good. Alicia Ford makes you stand at attention with her book, ***Echols From The Grave.*** Ford pours her soul out by taking you by the hand on a real-life journey, she walks you to the front door of the complexities of life, all while protecting the identities of those still living by using fictitious names. This family's history is amplified with secrets never-before revealed, until now.

Echol's From The Grave gives the audience an intimate look into an American family's life and archive in hope that a genuinely personal relevance is found on every page. Take your time, enjoy this literary masterpiece! This is an American story.

Foreword

I am pleased to write this foreword, on behalf of Alicia Ford (not only because she is beautiful, intelligent, bright, warm-hearted, giving, tenacious, and strong but) because she has poured her heart and soul into this writing to help someone catch their wave. I always knew there was something special about Mrs. Ford but couldn't figure it out until she shared a little of her past with me. Mrs. Ford's life resembled the narrative of the countless abused young women that I have provided services to for the past 20 years. I never knew that this divine connection between her and I was preparation for the journey that God envisioned for me.

The life afforded Mrs. Ford resembled the disturbances that ocean waves present (emotional trauma, sexual abuse, mental anguish), that was shaped by her unpleasant experiences. These embattled experiences led her on her journey of finding her "Echo" that would eventually begin her process of healing. Mrs. Ford uses the metaphor "Echo" to depict a wave, a radio frequency that one must catch to become part of the universe. Mrs. Ford followed the "Echo" and it led her to experience God's unwavering love, mercy, and grace.

Echols From The Grave speaks truth about the importance of finding your echo, your wave, your frequency in the God of this universe. Mrs. Ford experienced a level of trauma that could only be healed by God. She shared that God, our creator, is the epitome of "Love" and once you find it, your purpose in life becomes evident. Mrs. Ford found love in God, all while navigating through the rough terrain that the disturbance of the ocean presented.

Mrs. Ford found her "Echo" and began to ride the wave into the universe to find the purpose that God, the creator, intended for her. *Echols From The Grave* depicts how Mrs. Ford found her compass and it saved her life despite being born at a disadvantage (being poor, uneducated, and suffering physical and mental abuse) and lacking the morals to make sound choices and decisions.

This book is for anyone who is lost and does not feel worthy of love. I believe wholeheartedly that this story will provide you with insight on how to turn your trials into triumphs. Mrs. Ford was able to do just that and was lucky enough to bring calm to the waves to successfully navigate through in search of her "Echo". Echols From The Grave encourages you to "find your echo, your wave, your frequency. Never give up seeking until you catch your wave. Hear your echo. By all means, do yourself a favor: Never let go of God's love, mercy and grace." (Ford)

Dr. Catherine Nelson-Powell,
Founder and CEO
New Destiny Youth Facility, Residential Facility

Acknowledgment

I would like to acknowledge with sincere gratitude the following people and organizations.

Ms. Echols for her life and prayers to be answered for all her children. For the love, she imparted into my heart when she gave me my heartbeat.

Mr. and Mrs. S. for saying yes to God will for my life and their agape love and teaching me that with the faith of God can and will keep you. Just another day that Lord has kept me.

My beloved husband Bobby Ford for his unwavering love for God and his family and for covering us in God's word and prayer and being our provider.

To all of our children for your understanding that your mother is not perfect and I am blessed and highly favor to be your mother thank you for your support and belief in family.

Dr. Cathy Powell for her encouragement and leading by example that no one will be left behind.

The Salvation Army has fed and clothed so many in America in need.

The Volunteers of America and all adoption agency that has helped families become a family.

The National Domestic Violence organizations that still advocate for the rights of Americans to be heard and give voice to change.

Solano College Black Student Union Alumni.

Solano Office of Education Ms. Seratha Jefferson.

The Vallejo Omega Boys and Girls Club Mr. Pelton Stewart.

Lily of the Valley COGIC Bakersfield, California.

All my family and friends that have held me up in prayer and cheered me on Curry Brothers Publishing and staff for seeing the vision and not giving up on me.

Ms. Echols

What is the Real Meaning of Humanity?

An Echo is like a wave, a radio wave frequency, and when you learn to catch the wave, you become a part of the ocean, you become a part of the universe. If you are reading this, you are truly on the wave that The Creator, God, intended for you to be on!

On a Sunday morning, I sat in church, all dressed in white, ready for communion. The Prayer and Scripture had gone forth and the praise team had ushered in the spirit of the Lord. I was ready to receive the word of God. The Pastor started with, "'Going There' can't tell 'Been There' how to get there!"

At that moment, I was no longer a house plant in a pot getting upgraded to a bigger pot. I was now rooted and grounded in my spiritual walk with God. I received my blessing that day–it was the freedom to tell all those "Going There" that I had also "Been There" and with God's help they can (and will) "Get There" too! Unknowingly, COVID-19 would hit the world with a big punch and that would be the last day that we would fellowship in our beloved church building.

The weeks turned into months and Sunday services were now virtual. For over 20 years, our church was the one place we could run to during difficult times and devastation. Dedicated, daily my family read the Bible, hold prayer services virtually, sing praises unto

God. *Trusting in His Holy Word* that it will not come back void but will accomplish all that it was sent out to heal, set free, and make whole: mind, body, and soul.

I visited Ms. Echols' grave many times, always finding myself admiring the artwork and craftsmanship of her headstone, the inlay with a tree, the ocean, a sunset, and chestnuts that bordered the headstone. It was a thing of beauty.

After years of visiting, I finally saw the words that were engraved on the headstone. Given how often I went to visit, that may sound hard to believe but, up until that day, I never got past how peaceful the headstone looked.

The epitaph on Ms. Echols' headstone reads:
Ms. Echols
1933-1966
By Now The Angels Have Told Her
Why It Was Her Turn
And We All Must Die

As I looked through my teardrops, my heartbeat changed. The psychological blinders were coming off. I could hear my own heartbeat. It felt like thunder from heaven. I looked out into the sea of graves then back down. I heard Ms. Echols' echo from the grave through my own heartbeat; the one that she had given me. At this moment, I was one with The Creator. I was on the right wave at the right time. Not channel surfing, not in some in-between place, and not in a dead zone.

I am sharing with you the personal story of Ms. Echols and of her family. This is a universal story about God's Absolute Love. The characters' names have been altered to protect the identity of those still living but this is a story based on real peoples' lives. The following story takes place before there was a *#MeToo movement,* during a time when a single woman being murdered in her own home would not be a surprise.

Not only did Ms. Echols suffer from abuse but so did her mother, her daughter, and her granddaughters. This is why Ms. Echols represents any woman who was born poor and uneducated, who suffered abuse physically and mentally. The Ms. Echols of this world are always seeking and praying for a way out. Unfortunately for her, she had a lack of support, and no social network to depend on, but even when we look around today, we have more reports with statistics that show we still have a long way to go to help women like Ms. Echols!

According to the National Organization for Women (NOW), "1,181 women were murdered by an intimate partner in 2005*. That's an average of three women every day. Of all the women murdered in the U.S., about one-third were killed by an intimate partner."

Those who are economically disadvantaged are more likely to die from this type of abuse. Many turn a blind eye to the experiences of women like Ms. Echols, who suffer from their unheard echoes that are lost out at sea. What is the real meaning of humanity?

The definition of "human" is, 1. The entire **human race** or the characteristics that belong uniquely to human beings, such as kindness, mercy, and sympathy. An example of humanity is treating someone with kindness. 2. Human kindness, humanity to not only see and know the value of human life but ***the ability to cultivate that life.*** **

We are living in this social network now where everyone and anyone can be a part of it. Everyone cares more about being popular than being kind. That problem comes from disinformation and the lack of real help to catch the wave of humanity, to keep it going, to cultivate human life. It seems that people have become hell-bent on destroying humanity. It is as if the Human Race gets lost as we focus on the individual race of a person. God gave his love freely. We must become more compassionate to ourselves and one another.

My hope is that you can find your echo, your radio wave frequency and never give up seeking until you catch it.

Do yourself a favor, never let go of God's love, mercy, and grace. Hold on with every fiber of your being because I promise you that God's love is real.

1 Peter 4:8: "Above all, love each other deeply, because love covers a multitude of sins."

*1 Violence Against Women in the United States: Statistics
**2 Humanity Meaning | Best 14 Definitions of Humanity

Ms. Echols' Story

Dear Ms. Echols, The story starts with your father, Jack Echols. His United States World War I draft registration card describes him as red-headed, medium height with gray eyes. In 1917, he was 23 years old. That same year, on April 2, President Woodrow Wilson asked Congress to send United States troops into battle against Germany. In his address to Congress that day, Wilson lamented, "It is a fearful thing to lead these great peaceful people into the most terrible and disastrous of all wars..." Four days later, Congress obliged and declared war on Germany.

At first, Wilson asked only for volunteer soldiers, but he soon realized voluntary enlistment would not raise the sufficient number of troops required. In May 1917, he signed the Selective Service Act which mandated that all men between 21- and 35-years old register for the draft, increasing the size of the army from 200,000 troops to four million by the end of the war in 1918.

After the war, Jack was blessed to return home, where he married and started a family of his own. Jack's father had served in a war and his grandfather fought in the Civil War; the Echols men always served their country when called upon and they were always blessed to return home.

In 1917 your mother, Pearl Plazer, was only 11 years old. Six years later she and Jack were united in holy matrimony. Jack was 29 and she was 17. At that time, it was common for young women to marry older men. The Plazer family lost a daughter but gained a hard-working son, Jack Echols. 1923 was a very hot.

All German Ships Now in U. S. Ports Seized | HOME
FORT WORTH STAR-TELEGRAM | EDITION
FULL DAY ASSOCIATED PRESS REPORT BY LEASED WIRE

VOLUME XXXVII. NO. 64.   TWENTY-FOUR PAGES.   FORT WORTH, TEXAS, FRIDAY, APRIL 6, 1917.   PRICE 2 CENTS ON TRAINS 5 CENTS

WILSON SIGNS WAR DECREE

PROCLAMATION FORMALLY DECLARING BELLIGERENCY IS ISSUED BY PRESIDENT

WASHINGTON, Apr. 6.—President Wilson today signed the resolution of congress declaring a state of war between the United States and Germany.

Fort Worth Star-Telegram Newspaper ~1917

year in Texas and the young couple were off to a good start

In August 1929, the economy started to shrink. In October 1929, just a few years before you and your twin sister entered into the world, the stock market crashed. America was headed into the Great Depression. Then, a severe drought came upon the land which led to the Dust Bowl, destroying farms and obliterating finances.

Your father and mother were farmers and held on while so many others in the Midwest became homeless.

In 1933, the year you and Sally were born, the Great Depression had reached its lowest point and over 6,000 shanty towns popped up all over the Midwest. 15 million Americans were unemployed; families were devastated and unable to scrape up money for food. Breadlines and soup kitchens were established and there were so many homeless people that the lines would stretch across multiple blocks filled with desperate citizens struggling to get by. By this point, Pearl and Jack had been married for a good ten years and you had two older sisters: Fay and Janet. Jack worked on the farm and Pearl grew vegetables in her garden.

Impoverished family living in the Great Depression

The Great Depression was in full swing, and Jack had four daughters, but no son to help him on the farm. Texas and the rest of the United States were going through the Great Depression but it seemed the Echols' family had been going through hardships for quite a while. You and your sister, born on your mother's birthday, almost made it feel like a holiday in Seaton, Texas. It was your turn to enter into this world – to be born. In 1933, you and your identical twin sister, Sally Ann, decided to give your 27-year-old mother, Pearl, a birthday gift, one she would never forget!

Ms. Echols, your parents were both loving people who believed in God.

They tried their very best to give you more but life would offer hardships during The Dust Bowl for them. All you, even when there was no roof over your head, they loved you. They believed that God was love and love was God. When you and Sally were born in 1933 on your mother's birthday - they saw it as a blessing. A double blessing at that. Then, in 1935, you had a new sister, Barbara. Fay, your oldest sister, was now 10 years old and had been such a big help to her family. Even little Janet had been helping out. Having a baby is not easy but having four extra arms to help with the little ones came in handy for Pearl and Jack.

In addition to the Great Depression and Dust Bowl conditions, the Echols family would suffer even more tragedy: the loss of Fay from meningitis. The Stock Market Crash, the Dust Bowl, and the loss of your oldest sister Fay, at 12 years old, took its toll on the family. They were never the same. Now in his 40s, still young by today's standards, Jack's heart was broken from losing Fay and he never seemed to get past it. Fay reminded him of his many hopes and dreams when he was a young man back from the war, with a beautiful young wife, a beautiful baby, and land to work.

Everything all came crashing down like the stock market and blown away like the Dust Bowl. Jack never stopped loving his family, but as a man he felt like love was not enough to give; he was losing his hopes and dreams.

This would lead to Jack and Pearl breaking up; the drinking and fighting became too much. Sometimes this happens after the wedding vows. You have done all that you can to honor them and from nowhere, life throws your whole world upside down. Instead of holding on, you let go for survival's sake. You know that holding on will break you both wide open and nothing, and no one,

Pearl with her children:
Barbara, Sally, Ms. Echols, Fay

will survive the brokenness. There would be nothing left to put back together.

The Poor community was never fairly represented. The Poor did not have lawyers, due process of law, nor hand ups–just a lot of handouts. Privileged folks sit amongst each other and talk about how much money and material donations they had given to the poor. On Thanksgiving and Christmas, those same people volunteer to feed the hungry and provide toys to needy children.

The truth of the matter is, the poor still wake up poor! Ms. Echols, your father Jack gave the farm away for pennies to feed his family, just like so many others during the Dust Bowl and the Great Depression. Big oil companies were happy to pay pennies for the land and steal the mineral rights away from them because the farmer/ owner never knew anything about mineral rights. The poor will always be among us; the greedy will make sure of that.

Pearl, now a single mother with four kids, worked as often as she could when she could find work. You and Sally had to grow up quickly with no protection from the Hound Dogs that sniff out and seek little girls' souls to steal and destroy and kill their innocence. From time to time, Pearl and her young family often found themselves in the soup lines and in homeless shelters. Life for women during this time was very much dependent on men.

There was no welfare or food stamps available, no low income public housing, and no child care. Single women with children were often judged harsher than married women and single mothers who were not widowed were often scorned. Although President Franklin D. Roosevelt focused mainly on creating jobs for the masses of unemployed workers, he also backed the idea of federal aid for poor children and other dependent persons. By 1935, a national welfare system had been established for the first time in American history, but it would take years before every state was added into this process.

Pearl would marry again and have two more children; a son Earl, and a daughter Martha. Her second husband was a good provider for his new family and there seemed to be hope again. Your older sister Janet would soon marry and leave home. You and Sally looked up to her and would miss

*The Echols Girls (Twins Ms. Echols and Sally
with their younger sister, Barbara)*

her very much. Pearl was starting over with a new husband and two new children and Barbara was just young enough not to cause any problems. Pearl now had security for her family and respectability. There was now a place to call home with accessible food and new dresses, ribbons, and bows.

Ms. Echols, you and your twin, Sally, became beautiful young women; your ugly duckling days were far behind you. Your curly red hair and freckles were no longer the first thing people noticed when they saw you. Pearl's new marriage also offered the two of you the opportunity to continue your education. Sally enjoyed reading books and you liked to write. Books gave Sally a way to escape and that would eventually lead you and your identical twin very different roads.

Ms. Echols, you missed your father, Jack, greatly. Often, you felt abandoned. You questioned if all the fussing and fighting had anything to do with you. If you were not born, would it not happen? Would father not have left you? You spent much of your short-lived life trying to fill that hole in your heart. Did you find yourself looking for your father's love in all the wrong places? Were you looking for that unconditional love- someone who loved you for who you were (red hair, freckles, and all)?

The drinking and smoking made you appear a lot older. The Hound Dogs and Wolves in Sheep's Clothing would seek after you. Sally kept her nose in books and wasn't bothered by all of the attention because all she had to do was find someone to marry her and life would perhaps turn out like it was supposed to. At that time, the role model set for young women was to get married, be a good wife and mother, and make your husband's life a happy one and you would have a happy life too!

It was not like you didn't want a happy life with a loving husband. You wanted more than anything to be loved; however, your quest for love and affection would land you in reform school several times and you would be branded a sexual delinquent. The behavior of a sexual delinquent was defined by compulsive or repetitive acts indicating a disregard of consequences. In other words, an unmarried, pregnant minor. You, all of 16 years old, attending high school with a puppy-love boyfriend, did not understand the double standard that existed. Young men had no consequences for their compulsive or repetitive sexual acts, but young women did. Your mother Pearl most certainly did not want for you something that had been a difficult part in her life: raising a child without a husband.

Sometimes, first loves don't turn out the way you want: some are lucky in love and some are not. Your mother Pearl was lucky in love, unleashing her heart the first time out-the-gate. It was understandable that you believed things would turn out the same for you; your hopes and dreams of having that unconditional love were now real and you were happy for the first time in your very young life. You absolutely glowed during your pregnancy with Steve, and you were not ashamed of the life that grew inside of you.

When you could, you and Sally worked odd jobs to buy the little necessities of life. Pearl was no longer married and money was held fist-tight. In 1865, the same year the Civil War ended in America, the Salvation Army was established in London, England. By 1880 the organization had moved into the United States. The Salvation Army was a big part of your life, providing you with food and shelter. Another organization would become a big part of your life:

The Volunteers of America, established in 1896. They offered maternity homes and adoption services for unwed mothers.

Ms. Echols, bless your soul! You never thought that having a baby and keeping the baby would be such an impossibility. After all, you believed in God. You believed that He could do the impossible and make a way for you and your child. You would finally have something and someone of your own to love and someone to love you back. Pearl and the Volunteers of America would help you and support you with the adoption of Steve. As his mother, you wanted what was best for your child and adoption would be better than an orphanage. You could finish high school (something Pearl never had the opportunity to do) and perhaps one day the right man would come along, marry you, and give you a family to love and you would be loved in return.

Ms. Echols, I know you were confused and had lost the ability to trust, hope, or dream. What was not explained to you was that after having your baby Steve, after nursing him the first few days of his life, a bond had taken place. What they did not tell you, Ms. Echols, is that it would take a few months before your breast milk would dry up. You were supposed to forget everything that happened and go on with your life, like it never happened at all. You were committed to a mental hospital and sent to Gainesville State School for Girls for 23 months, almost two years of your young life.

Teenagers of the 1950s began exerting a growing influence on American life and commerce. The rapid rise of this growing demographic had unleashed a wave of anxiety among adults. It was a fear both real and imagined. The number of crimes committed by teenagers was, in fact, rising throughout the nation. There was also a level of intense

Pearl and Ms. Echols at Gainesville's Reformation School

anxiety that seemed unwarranted concerning the new power of the emerging teen demographic. Teenagers seemed to be challenging the social fabric of America. Many questioned and even blamed movies, comic books, and Rock and Roll for their bad influence on the rising misbehavior of youth.

The State of Texas was mostly unsuccessful in trying to turn bad girls into good girls. Gainesville State School for Girls was established in 1913 as a home for delinquent dependent girls. Girls between the ages of eight and seventeen were sent to the institution by a court order. Originally called the Texas State Training School for Girls, the school was authorized by the 33rd Legislature, which had appropriated $25,000 for construction. Under the direction of its first superintendent, Dr. Carrie Weaver Smith (1916–1925), the school sought to rehabilitate delinquent girls and stressed character building, formation of habits of self-control and stability, better understanding of spiritual values, and an ability to cope with present social conditions, as well as providing an education that emphasized vocational skills. The school, located on a 160-acre tract just east of Gainesville, Texas began with four dormitories and a superintendent's residence. By 1948, when enrollment reached 198, it took on its present name, Gainesville State School for Girls. At that time, the campus included seven brick cottages, five frame houses for the families of staff members and several other buildings including a gymnasium, a hospital, a school building with a cafeteria and an auditorium, a beauty parlor, and a laundry. From the beginning, the school had been relatively self-sufficient; food for the girls and staff was grown on portions of the land.

Males were not sent to Gainesville State Schools or mental hospitals for getting a girl pregnant and there was no child support collected from them. In a pregnancy, their reputations stayed intact and only the girl's reputation was ruined. After all, good girls did not have children out-of-wedlock. Good girls were to speak when spoken to and never, ever question authority.

From reformation school, you learned about not displaying your emotions associated with having a baby and giving it up. You learned to hide your real feelings and were told to keep your thoughts and opinions to yourself - nobody wants a Know-It-All Nancy. They taught you to be a pretty girl who would do what she is told to do, when she is told to do it. Somehow everything was always your fault because you were a bad girl. Look at where you were living. Only

16

bad people ended up in places like Gainesville State School; people who I am sure had done worse things than have a baby-out-of- wedlock. Funny thing though Ms. Echols, the condom had been around for some time. Contraceptives existed but were not easily accessible - some believe the condom was invented by Charles Goodyear in America in 1839 and patented in 1844. Other accounts attribute it to Thomas Hancock in Britain in 1843. Regardless of the inventor, the first rubber condom was produced in 1855 and by the late 1850s several major rubber companies were mass-producing them.

Ms. Echols, Steve had a wonderful life growing up. He was raised by loving, kind-hearted people who gave him everything you never could - a strong foundation to build his own life and a family unit of his own. He never went without the basic necessities: food, shelter, clothes on his back and shoes on his feet. His adopted parents loved him with the kind of love you would want for him. He grew up to be a happy, loving, and kind man. Steve had his questions of course, like most folks who find out years later that the parents who raised him and loved him were not his biological parents and they did it because they wanted to, not because they had to. Steve now has three children and has been married to his wife for 44 years. He has an awesome sense of humor and was so happy to have found out that you were his mom. He was thankful that you did right by him. You gave him a chance to be all that you knew he could be, even when he got lost in his younger years, he always had love in his heart.

The Volunteers of America

Ms. Echols, I know it wasn't easy for you and you were still searching for love. Then, along comes Lily's father who asked you to marry him. You, at 18, would finally find happiness in your life. Sally was also soon to be married. You could hear the wedding bells for Sally as you waited your turn. Sally got married and for the first time, you identical twins began to live a life apart from each other, but you were still connected to each other's thoughts, feelings, and emotions. You and Sally were very happy young women, both with babies in your bellies. There was one exception. You were waiting on your man who would return to keep his promise of marriage. He would soon be back from the oil rig, and you could start your own home together and fill it with love.

"Roughneck" is a term for a person who works on an oil rig and roughnecks were very plentiful in Texas boomtowns with the discovery of black gold. Life as a roughneck oil rig worker was dangerous but it paid good money - $150 a week compared to the $30 dollars a week you made as a waitress in Texas during the 1950s.

The following letter was sent to the Social Services Department, Big Springs State Hospital, Big Springs, Texas, dated August 1951, from The Volunteers of America and has been reproduced from its redacted form. A letter I am sure you had never seen before:

Dear Mrs. Hale,

Your letter on August 8th was a surprise to us. We had Ms. Echols as a patient from April 1949, until her dismissal in July 1949. In July 1949, a boy was born. He was left for adoption and placed in August 1949. Mrs. Plazer knew her daughter was with us because she wrote several times. The girl came to us but soon after she was committed to the Texas School for sex delinquency.

Ms. Echols was a discipline problem with us, but not a health problem. The baby appeared to be normal. The couple were told that [the baby's] father was a hospital case. They did not feel that would have any bearing on their child.

Can you tell us the diagnosis and prognosis in the case of this girl? Is she a 90-day voluntary commitment or is she there for longer?

You might be interested to know that her older sister has recently been discharged from our home. She was legally married, but illegitimately pregnant. She kept her baby and is supposed to be living there in Texas. She was not the discipline problem that Ms. Echols was, but she was very moody and depressed. She had less personality than Ms. Echols.

If I can be of further service to you, please call on us.

Sincerely,

The Volunteers of America

20

No more letters would follow until November 1951.
Ms. Echols wrote:

Dear Mrs. Lockney, [sic]
I am going to have my baby in February, and I am not married. I have worked as long as I can, and I would like to come down there. I don't know if you remember me or not, but I have been down there before. I could come next Friday. Let me know right away so I can come.

Thanking you,
Ms. Echols

A reply to Ms. Echols letter was sent from The Volunteers of America, dated November 1951:

Dear Ms. Echols,
We received your letter today asking for admittance to The Volunteers of America Maternity Home. Have you had a physical check-up from your doctor? We would very much like to have his report, either in advance or when you come.

We do have a vacancy and can admit you in November, during the office hours listed in the folder. Please fill out the application and bring [it] with you if you come on this date, or mail if coming later.

If adoption of the baby is your plan, we will hold a place for you. Our office will be closed tomorrow and only one worker is here on Friday; but she can talk with you in our office before going home.

Yes, we remember you as a former patient and in accepting a patient for the second time, we must be assured [of] the very best cooperation while in the home. It will be best if your previous stay in the home is not mentioned to the other girls for now. We have a fine group of girls and a wonderful staff – some you know, others are new. We will give you the best care we possibly can.

Yours most sincerely,
The Volunteers of America

These are the report notes from The Volunteers of America, dated November 1951. The specific name of the person working with Ms Echols is unknown and will be called "The Worker" as the following is reproduced from the redacted document:

Ms. Echols arrived by Greyhound bus around 5:00 P.M. and called the Volunteers of America office. She was informed to leave her baggage and come to the office in the Majestic Building for information and then a worker would take her to the home and get her baggage on the way.

Ms. Echols (a former patient in 1949) was in the office about 15 minutes later. She was dressed neatly with low heeled black oxfords, a navy-blue skirt, short green coat, white blouse, and her pretty red hair was neatly combed. Ms. Echols was rather nervous as the worker talked with her and when asked about the putative father she started to cry and said, "I could just kill myself if I cry." She hesitated and said, "He is a roughneck and is dead." The worker asked if he was killed in an accident, and she said yes but had no other reply. The worker, noting that Ms. Echols was nervous and hesitant, decided not to get further information and instead took her to the home until she relaxed. Ms. Echols's actions could have been a feeling of shame in coming back to the Volunteers of America for a second time. Her sister was also in the Volunteers of America home. She kept her baby and left in July 1951.

The worker asked Ms. Echols about her plans regarding the baby, and she said she didn't know but wanted to think the matter over. The worker pointed out that the financial arrangement was somewhat different if a girl kept her baby. The Organization would have to look to her for some of her care and the baby's. The worker also referred to the letter written to her about coming to the home that stated IF ADOPTION is your plan, we have a vacancy. Two- or three-times Ms. Echols mentioned that she needed to THINK. Ms. Echols had been working as a waitress.

The worker took Ms. Echols (who will be called "Nancy" while in the Home) to the Home where she was introduced to Mrs. Vance and the girls. She had supper and quickly became part of the group, as she joined the girls on the back porch for a "smoke" after supper. She was escorted to her room by one of the girls and seemed to feel at home, again.

The volunteer's of America's Lt. Major wrote that,

Ms. Echols acted as though she could not control herself if [she] talked much. The Lt. Major talked with her briefly, saying she could go to [the] home without a definite decision re: the baby but she should let us know soon and if [she] decided to keep the baby, let us know immediately as we would have to make different arrangements.

She couldn't decide on a nickname, so it was suggested by The Worker to call her "Nancy" from a nice girl she used to care for in Lubbock and who reminded her of Ms. Echols. They took her to [the] Maternity Home. The Lt. Major, of the Volunteers of America Maternity Home, in Fort Worth, Texas, as an application form and history sheet, dated December 1951, containing Ms. Echols's personal information is summarized and paraphrased from the redacted copy as follows:

Name: Nancy.
Present Age: 18.
Nationality: Scottish, Irish, and German.
Religion: Protestant - Baptist. Joined the church at age 13. No church activity.

Physical Appearance: Height, 5' 7." Normal weight, 140 lbs. Complexion, fair with freckles. Color of eyes, brown. Hair, red-wavy (pretty). Shape of face, square, nice. Nose, medium. Eyes, large. Very thick lips. Ears small. Hands long and slender. Feet size 8. Healthy, well-nourished normal development, average, attractive, clean, nice form, excellent posture.

Remarks: Nancy came by bus by appointment near closing time, dressed fairly neat but nervous and emotionally upset. Undecided about the baby. Nancy is a nice-looking girl especially when dressed up.

Health: Condition of sight, good. Hearing, good. Teeth, irregular but good. Heart, OK. Stomach, OK. General Physical Condition: Good, very healthy appearing. History of Diseases: Measles, mumps, chicken pox, whooping cough.

Education: High School 11th grade, "B" average. Favorite subject, history.

Typing 75-80 words. Could have taken while in Gainesville State School for Girls: beauty, secretary, or nursing classes. Nancy regrets she did not avail herself of the opportunity of courses offered while she was in Gainesville State School for Girls for 23 months.

Personality: Nancy is probably high average.

Mentality: Average, nervous (smokes incessantly, smoked marijuana 2 to 4 months in 1949), pure-minded, slightly evil-minded.

Characteristics: Sly, bold, trusting, cynical, charming, ordinary. Dresses ordinary, looks nice in browns and greens. Interests: Skating, motorcycling, reading books, basketball. Likes to cook but doesn't sew.
Occupation: Waitress for six months at $30 dollars a week plus tips before coming to Volunteers of America. Home Life Environment: Rented. Relatives, a stepfather with sister Janet. "I've always had a rugged home life," she said in tears. Mother had been arrested three times. Father in VA hospital with his brother. Nancy lived in a small apartment two months before coming to Volunteers of America with a former client of Volunteers of America, who kept her baby and is having hard times, but wants Nancy to keep this baby. Only one family member who wants her to. Social Status: Unmarried.

Children born previously: One (male).

Social Status at Time of Birth: Single.

Detail of Children: Sex, male. Living, yes. Health, OK good. Education & whereabouts, placed for adoption by Volunteers of America. He is fine physically and above average mentally. Adoptive parents have a new home now. (See Record #1).

Previous Sex Experience: Rather promiscuous, one pregnancy.

Pages 4 & 5 – Volunteers of America Maternity Home, Application Form and History Sheet, December 1951, contains Confidential Family History of Client's Mother and Father. (Not included here).

Page 6 – Continued Volunteers of America Maternity Home, Application Form and History Sheet, December 1951:

Girl's Story: Nancy met the father in April 1951 and knew him for four months. He was killed at Vincent Field as a rigger-derrick man. She didn't know him very well and knew very little about his family.

Confidential Information of Putative Father:
Age: 24.
Nationality: Irish - German.
Religion: Unknown.
Education: Unknown.
Occupation: Where employed, blank. Capacity, Oilfield. How long, blank. Rate of pay, $310 every two weeks.
Physical appearance: Height, 6' 2." Normal weight, 190 lbs., Complexion, light. Color of eyes, blue. Color of hair: blond. Shape of face: square with deep dimples. Teeth: good.
General Appearance: Blank.

Health: Hearing, sight, teeth, heart, stomach, all checked off. General physical condition, good so far as Nancy knows. He smoked a pipe and drank liquor.

Personality: He was easy going, quiet, clean.

Interests: Liked to dance and see movie shows. Football. Social Status: Unmarried, deceased.

Statement by Putative Father as quoted by girl: Knew of baby, but not interested.

Identity of Putative Father established beyond a reasonable doubt? Yes.

All other questions blank except the putative father had an older sister who was a car dealer.

A letter was written to the Volunteers of America from Pearl Plazer, Ms. Echols's mother, dated February 1952, before the baby was born:

Dear Madam,

I'm Mrs. Pearl Plazer, Ms. Echols' Mother. I feel like I should write to you but am afraid I might say the wrong thing. I've tried to stand by and help Ms. Echols all I could but with money I just never have much. I've been working but make very little and right now I'm not working. I hurt my arm and will have to be off for a few weeks. I can't say how long.

Ms. Echols can work and make enough to just get along if she is careful, but I don't know how she thinks she could support a baby and get a reliable person to care for it on what she'll make. I'd like for her to have this baby so much if it would help her be satisfied but as things are, it is very hard to get by without a husband to help and alone it is next to impossible. If there is any way that you could avoid letting her know I told you this, please do so. It would make it hard on me and her when she comes home. Make her see she has to leave her baby there until she has a good job and everything ready to care for it. I tried every way I could to talk her into giving the baby a good chance at life, but she can't seem to see it that way.

Resp.
Mrs. Pearl Plazer

That would be the last letter written to the Volunteers of America regarding Ms. Echols and her babies.

Ms. Echols, I am so sorry that no one ever asked you what you wanted and if you were okay. You would be released from the Volunteers of America in early March 1952. Your baby, Lilly, would grow up in a loving family and have a good life, not a rugged life like yours. Lilly would be married and have one child, a daughter, and work for the Government for many years. She was very grateful for her life and wanted you to know she was a happy person. She thanked you for doing right by her. Lilly's adopted family gave her a good life.

Wildflower

In May of 1952, you went to live with your older sister Janet and her husband and family. You worked odd jobs and helped her with household duties when you could. You looked up to her. Even if they did not have much, they had each other. However, you did not plan for your stay to include accommodating her husband. In his eyes you were a pretty, young wildflower that had not had sex the right way with the right man. He tried to tame you. You eventually became pregnant by him and had to run away. You couldn't tell anyone because who would believe you and your side of the story? You couldn't break up a happy home. You knew the people to contact, and you knew what you would have to do. Joy, your third baby and second daughter, was born in 1953. She would also be adopted. Later, your daughter Joy, who loved to sing Rock & Roll and ride motorcycles, would have two daughters of her own.

You found your twin sister, Sally, and explained everything to her. She was the one person who never passed judgment on you. She loved you no matter what. Sally was just starting a family; she had two young sons. You did not want to be in a similar situation again. You knew you would have to leave as soon as possible. Your reputation of being easy and someone who "could be had by any man" was all they talked about in the family. Ms. Echols, you were the *"wild child"*, who had had three babies and no man. Thinking to yourself, *No good man would ever take you for a wife.*

That was until you met a man, Mr. D. He was a recent widower, who was still grieving. You knew all, too well, about heartache and pain. He talked about moving to California. The West was the place to be! You could be far enough away that your bad reputation would stay in Texas and not follow you. Mr. D married you and you spent your honeymoon driving to California with the hopes and dreams that it was going to be okay. You could have your own family for you to love and have love given back.

Ms. Echols, you became Mrs. D and had Baby number four, a girl, April, born in 1954. There was not a need for the Volunteers of America, nor an adoption. Then, another girl, Lisa, arrived in 1955. Your sixth child was your son, Jack, born in 1956. You gave birth to Baby number seven, Bobby, born in 1957. The eighth, David, was born in 1958 and baby number nine, Rose, in 1959. You were 26 years old and happy! You were a loving mother to your babies. Your photos showed you smiling at the world. Like your mother, there was not a lot of money and not a lot of help with all those babies.

You were married to Mr. D in name-only. If not for the baby-making part, you could never replace his former wife. First, you had red hair. Second, he was Hispanic and you didn't know his culture very well. It was enough for you but not enough for him. You told Mr. D everything about your past and everything that you shared with him, he would use against you.

After your services were no longer needed, Mr. D would bring in the woman he wanted to be near his children. You knew nothing about his culture and you could never rear his children the right way, his way.

Ms. Echols

He would remind you of your past whenever he
wanted to hurt you and break you down. Even after all
of the beatings you endured, you still stayed with him for
your babies' sake. You did not know that Mr. D would put
you out on the street like a dog and dare you to return.
He told each of your children that you were a red-headed
witch that could never be trusted. You tried to stay close,
working right up the street from the house where you had
lived with them. You lived in a tiny room in the back of a

house close by just so you could from time to time. When you happened to run into them in a public park, he would forbid you from speaking to them and he told them to run away from the redheaded witch.

Ms. Echols, life was not very kind to you. Even though Mr. D was done with you, he hated to see you with other men. Finding yourself pregnant, again, was another nail in your coffin. He did not want you, but he didn't want you with anyone else either.

Ms. Echols, you were really at rock-bottom. Sleeping with black men in the 1960s was taboo. In many states it was illegal for Black and White people to even marry. The three black men that were your lovers were kind to you and did not try to tame you in any way. They had no need to beat you, so it was very understandable why you began to trust them. Married men were safer for you to trust. No more heartbreaks with promises of marriage, no dissolution of marriage with no kids. Two of your lovers were brothers and became your friends; their family enjoyed your company and liked having you around. You learned not to talk too much about your past because people might use it against you. You did not expect to have a "happily ever after." You weren't seeking love anymore, just some kindness and humanity. One brother was married with four kids and one was married with no kids.

Ms. Echols, you were 27 years old in 1960, pregnant with your tenth child, due in 1961. The man with eight kids would have nothing to do with you anymore. His hands were full dealing with his own family, and he loved his wife and kids very much. He was just being kind to you and perhaps he got caught up in the moment. The man with four kids loved his wife and kids too, but he had a bigger heart, one that could give a little more to someone who needed love and wanted to be loved. He would continue to try to help you and he believed he was possibly the father of your baby. He told his brother about your pregnancy, and he also told his wife and sisters.

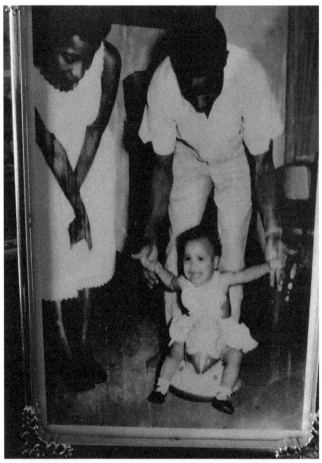

The family Josephine was gifted to, Mr. & Mrs. S

Josephine's Story

Dear Ms, Echols, I was born in the Summer of 1961. Running and hiding to save yourself was hard enough; but with a baby, it was much more difficult. You tried to keep me for as long as possible. You took me with you to Casa Loma Creek to hide from the beatings. The Winter season was exceptionally cold and you felt that Christmas would be a special time to gift me to Mr. & Mrs. S. They were friends. The man was a candidate as to who you believed was my father. You would be able to see me periodically. The couple gave me a home filled with love and provided the things you never had and could never give. The husband and wife came together and accepted me into their family. Though it was not a formal adoption, they did not speak about you being my mother. Mr. & Mrs. S would now be my parents and the affair was never to be acknowledged.

You named me after my second great-grandmother on your mother's side of the family. She was Josephine Blake, born in 1852 in Marshall, Mississippi. Her father, William, lived to be 46 years old, and her mother, Sarah, was 42 when she died. Josephine married Isaiah Edward Plazer in 1869, in Shreveport, Louisiana, when she was 17 years old. They had 18 children in 26 years. She died in 1918 when she was 65 years old.

Baby-makin' was in our genes. At the time there was not easily accessible birth control besides condoms and there wasn't any information on abortion. Children often died during birth or as infants, as an agrarian society, having a big family was necessary to help with the planting and growing crops of America. Ms. Echols, I was chip-off-the-block, Wild Child, just like you. Our country was changing and people were beginning to feel like there was hope for mankind.

In 1961, John F. Kennedy (JFK) was inaugurated as the 35th president of the United States and change for humanity seemed possible. The Freedom Riders rode buses into the Southland to bravely challenge Jim Crow Laws of segregation. Troops were being deployed to Vietnam.

Ms. Echols, I was now 2 years old and Mr. S and Mrs. S moved from Bakersfield to Los Angeles for better job opportunities for Mr. S. We often visited Bakersfield as it was only an hour away over the Grapevine.

When Mr. & Mrs. S would try to find you to check on you, they would ask around and hear gossip about you through the Bakersfield Grapevine, which was how news traveled in Bakersfield at that time. The reports about you were not good. Mr. & Mrs. S heard that men, old flames and new, had beaten you down. Domestic Violence against women was not yet considered a "real" crime back then. Some women still believed it was a man's way of showing his love. They would say: "He beat me because he loved me, that's all, he loves me, and he doesn't mean nothing by it."

The Majestic Fox Theatre during the prime days of the '50s

Ms. Echols, in 1964 you were seven months pregnant with baby number eleven, Anna, when you contacted the Department of Human Services. There had been a big fight over Mr. D - he was engaged to another woman and wanted a divorce. You were quite angry about this and ended up spending a year in jail for assault with a deadly weapon used on "the other woman." Your jail time gave you the opportunity to write short stories and you made attempts to get them published. Although these attempts were not successful, you did receive nice compliments from some of the publishers.

Anna's father was 30-something. He was a friendly guy, about 5' 11 and weighed around 175 pounds with dark olive skin, dark hair and dark eyes. He worked in construction and was a veteran, but he was not supportive of you when he learned of the baby. You believed that adoption was the best thing for Anna.

Ms. Echols, it seemed like we were coming to Bakersfield more often, almost every other weekend, and I remembered one visit close to the 4th of July, 1966. I had started school in Los Angeles, but I liked our family trips to Bakersfield where there were other kids to play with. While outside playing in the hot sun, one of the kids said to me, "That white woman, that is your real momma. She is working at that cafe around the corner."

It was not the first time one of the kids that I played with would make some off-the-wall remark to me about who I was and who I was not. Remarks about me being a "half-breed" or a "mixed mutt". By the time I started going to school, I became more aware of comments about myself.

I decided to jump on a bike that was lying on the ground. I went around the corner to see you for myself. I knew I was not supposed to go but I couldn't help myself.

I rode up to look through the window of the cafe. I could not see anyone eating; it looked like no one was in the place. I thought the kids had led me on a wild goose chase, and I was mad! They would all get a good laugh when I came riding back.

I turned around to look in the back of the cafe and then I saw you, Ms. Echols, standing there. I dropped the bike right at the front door and I walked in like I had money to buy something. You were looking at me and I was looking at you. Pulling myself up to the counter, I sat down. You were peeling potatoes and smiling at me. You asked me if I would like some ice cream. Of course, I said yes. I was eating my ice cream and taking the skins from the potatoes and eating them too. You asked me if I liked them, and I said yes. You said, "Me too" and we both laughed out loud. I remembered how I felt on the inside, a feeling that was good – I felt joy. Then, one of the kids came running in and yelled at me. He said, "You're in trouble, you're going to get it, bring your own switch." They all ran off and took the bike to make sure it would take me even longer to get back to my awaited fate.

Ms. Echols, that moment in the cafe meant the world to me.Nothing and no one could ever take that one moment in time away from us. I still hold it dear to my heart. You were happy to see me, and I was happy to see you. This was a moment of happiness for two people who did not have a lot of happy moments. Our hug at the end made it feel like everything was going to be alright and everything was just as it should be. There was peace. No sadness, just love and lots of happiness and overwhelming joy. No questions asked, no judgments, no expectations, no fakeness, just one precious moment in time.

I took my time and walked back slowly, trying to hold on to those joyous feelings but when I walked back, Mr. & Mrs. S were already in the car waiting for me and ready to go. Mrs. S was fussing about something, so I climbed in the back seat and looked out the window with a big smile at the other kids. I was saved! The other kids did not get the pleasure of watching me get into trouble. We left the part of Bakersfield, known to be a good area because they had sidewalks, and drove to another area of Bakersfield that had no sidewalks, just dirt. Here most people kept chickens in their backyards and had gardens. Most of the men wore overalls but some looked like cowboys from Western movies.

When we arrived, one of Mr. S's sisters was standing out in front of her house crying and yelling at us to go and get Ms. Echols. Mr. & Mrs. S went inside the house with his sister to talk. Kids always had to stay outside when we went to Bakersfield but we were not allowed to play in the front yard. We had to stay in the backyard, so I walked around to the backyard, still feeling pretty good on the inside and there was a boy I knew. He was about my age, maybe a few years older. We would often play together, and he had recently been to Los Angeles and stayed with us. I remember because he gave me chicken pox which fortunately, I did not get as bad as he did. I often thought, Whose bright idea was it to have him stay with us and give me the chicken pox? He could be mean to me, or he could be nice. I was just waiting to see what he was going to say to me that day.

I always tried to get in the house to hear what the adults were talking about. A child was only allowed in the house to eat and/or use the bathroom, so I remembered turning on the water hose in the back yard and drinking water from the hose. The boy ran behind me and pushed me away and said, "It's my turn". I chased him all over the backyard because he pushed me and took the water hose from me. We were having fun making the best of our time outside then I said, "I'm going in. I need to pee." He said, "You better not go in there, I know what you're trying to do. You want to hear what they're talking about. I know what you are trying to do. They told me to keep you out here and if you have to pee, well, just go behind the shed or something."

I began to cry. Crying would always make the adults come running. He told me to shut up before he got in trouble because they thought he had hit me or something. He said, "I'll tell you what they're talking about if you would just stop crying, you little crybaby." He was right, I was a crybaby and a tattle-tell and that meant most of the kids did not like me very much. I wanted to be close to the back door just in case it opened so I could run inside, so we sat down on the back steps. He said, "That white woman has been calling my momma all week crying about some man who was going to kill her, and she needed Mr. S to come over right away." I did not know many white people and whenever somebody was talking about "that white woman" they were always talking about you, Ms. Echols. They never called you by your name, it was always just "that white woman."

My heart was racing now, and I could hear the telephone ringing in the house. I was thinking that it was "that white woman" calling, crying into the phone, saying that the man was trying to KILL her. When was somebody going to answer the damn phone? It kept ringing and ringing.

The boy was still talking but for some reason I just saw his mouth moving; I couldn't hear anything coming out of his mouth. I stood up and banged on the back door crying out to let me in, let me in, then took off running to the front of the house because I knew the front door was open; it was always open. The boy was running behind me saying, "Wait! You're going to get us in trouble!" It's funny how as kids we often thought if one child gets in trouble, we all would get in trouble.

Mr. & Mrs. S and his sister were headed towards the car, and they seemed to be in a hurry. I ran and jumped into the car and looked out the window at the boy like I had just won a race and came in first place. The boy knew not to get into the car, so he stopped, stood there and looked at me with an "I told you so" expression. Mr. S drove off really fast. Whenever he would drive really fast, I would lie down on the floor behind the seat. Even if I was lying down on the floor, I could feel the car going up the mountain over the grapevine. Wherever we were going, it was not over the grapevine. The car stopped and all three adults jumped out in a hurry. I heard them calling out "Ms. Echols! Ms. Echols! Ms. Echols, are you in there?" Then Mr. S's sister knocked hard on the door. I peeked my head up and looked from the backseat.

To my surprise, I saw the house where I had been before and thoughts of the white lady at the cafe came into my head. This was her house. I was happy once more thinking I was going to see her again, twice in one day! I could see Mr. & Mrs. S looking into a yellow-curtained window. These were the same yellow curtains I remembered from before, the ones I thought made the tiny house look alive. But the curtains were different now, they seemed to be hanging down and they looked ragged, missing the life they had brought to the tiny little house.

I jumped out of the car and started running towards the house with arms wide open, hopeful that the redheaded, freckle-faced white lady was going to come out to grab me up and hug me.

Mrs. S turned around and saw me running and she started towards me with tears in her eyes. She grabbed me and took me back to the car. We sat there in the car crying. I was crying because she was crying. Then Mr. S and his sister headed to the car, and they were crying too. Everybody in the car was crying. We sat for a while then someone said, "What are we going to do?" Mr. S said, "I don't know what to do, we were too late." I thought to myself, we were driving very fast, how can we be too late?

The two women were hugging each other and sobbing. As I sat in his lap, Mr. S just kept looking at the house with tears in his eyes. I had never seen someone's eyes look so sad. He held me close to him and said, "You don't have to worry, I am going to take care of you and nothing and nobody will ever hurt you." I felt safe but I was very sad. On the inside, my heart was hurting. Mr. S said to the two women that we would have to get out of there; there was nothing we could do. We were too late, Ms. Echols was dead. Mr. S told his sister that while she was knocking on the door, he had looked through the window and saw Ms. Echols lying on the bed, dead. Her eyes were open but rolled back in her head. We were too late.

The infamous Bakersfield Sign on Union Ave. ~ 1960

4th of July

It was July 4th 1966, and I was barely 5 years old. We drove back to Mr. S's sister's house very slowly and I saw the boy still standing where we had left him. We all sat in the car with tears streaming down our faces. The boy walked up to the car, looked at our faces and the tears in our eyes, but did not say anything. Mrs. S and Mr. S's sister got out of the car holding onto each other and trying to hold one another up as they walked slowly to the house. Mr. S sat in the car crying really hard once the women were gone. I wanted to comfort him so I sat in his lap again and told him everything was going to be okay; I would take care of him. He looked at me and smiled a little. He asked me if I needed to use the restroom before we got on the road. He said he would take me back to Los Angeles and leave me with his other sister for a couple of days. He told me to be a good girl and he would be back soon to get me. The women were still crying when we walked into the house. Mr. S said he and Mrs. S would take me back to Los Angeles then they would return to Bakersfield.

The drive up the grapevine seemed to make me sick. I often got car sick and by the time we had made it to Gorman they had to pull over. I still didn't understand what was going on, but Mr. & Mrs. S were having a discussion when I got back to the car. Mrs. S did not want to leave me in Los Angeles but Mr. S said it was for the best because they did not have papers for me. If they called the police and told them Ms. Echols was dead, I might be taken from them. I still did not understand what they were talking about. I sat up front right next to both of them. (Because of the car sickness, Mr. & Mrs. S often gave me a little sip of beer to help me sleep when we were driving.) I must have fallen asleep in the car but then I woke up in a wet bed. I was afraid I would get in trouble for wetting the bed. I then realized where I was; in Los Angeles with Mr. S's sister. I got up to go to the restroom but I was also afraid of the dark and it was dark outside and the room was dark.

I stood in the room, crying with my mouth wide open, getting louder and louder so someone would come to get me. The door opened and a light came on. Mr. S's sister looked at me, opened her arms and said, "It's okay, don't cry." She could see that I had wet the bed, so she took me by my hand and led me to the bathroom. She filled the tub and poured a bubble bath usingMr. Bubbles™ (my favorite!) into the water. Only at her house did I get to have bubble baths.

I loved Mr. S's sister. She was pretty and nice to me. She had a job, her own car, her own house and she was so much fun to be with. We were always dancing. She had a husband, who looked like a white man, but he talked funny. The family did not call him a white man like they would call you, Ms. Echols, a white woman. He was Cuban but to me he just looked like a white man. He would play the bongos every time there was a get-together with music and dancing, and he was nice to me too. If I would get afraid when I stayed the night, they would let me climb into the bed with them and I felt safe.

After the bath, I asked her if it was still the 4th of July. She smiled and said there were a few more moments left. She grabbed my clothes off the floor and threw them into the tub and said, "Help me wash your things so you can have something to wear tomorrow." It was fun and my clothes smelled like Mr. Bubbles. She said, "Let's hurry up, there are only a few minutes left on the 4th of July." She gave me a big, oversized tee shirt that looked like a long gown on me and took me by the hand as we went outside to a small grassy area. She handed me a sparkler and asked if I wanted her to help me light it. I told her I was afraid but she said she would help me. Mr. S's sister took the sparkler out of my hand and lit it. My eyes got big and I started backing up while she was walking towards me. She kneeled down and then I came closer. She walked behind me and placed her hands around my hands, and we held it together until it went out.

When we went back into the house, the bed was clean and my clothes were draped over the door. She said, "Let's say our prayers before we go to bed. Repeat after me: Now I lay me down to sleep, I pray The Lord my soul to keep, if I should die before I wake, I pray The Lord my soul to take. God bless mommy and God bless daddy and God bless Ms. Echols. Amen." I remember laying there thinking the words of the prayer over and over until I fell asleep.

A few days went by before Mr. & Mrs. S returned to pick me up. They came in Mr. S's old green work truck, and he was even more upset than the last time I saw him. Mr. & Mrs. S, his sister and I went to a wrecking yard and there was Mr. S's white Thunderbird all smashed up. When I saw the car, (I don't know what happened to me) but I freaked out. I started crying uncontrollably and it was like I forgot how to speak. Every time I tried to open my mouth to talk, it came out in a really bad stutter. I felt all smashed up on the inside just like that Thunderbird. A deep sadness and fear was taking root inside my heart.

Mr. S had let someone else drive his car and they had had a very bad accident. We had to drive back to Bakersfield because one person in the Thunderbird had died from the wreck. I was not looking forward to going to Bakersfield again because I now stuttered, and the other kids would make fun of me.when visiting Bakersfield, the black kids made it hard on me. In Bakersfield I did not know any white people except Ms. Echols. In Bakersfield, every house was owned by black people, every corner store, night club, and church was owned by black people. I would not be able to speak up for myself and they would say I was faking it for attention. I don't think anybody understood how painful it was for me when I tried to speak. The sorrow caused me pain as I tried to get words out of my mouth.

Living in Los Angeles was very copacetic in the 1960's made me feel brand new; kids did not pick on me or call me half-breed or mixed mutt.

At my school there were other kids and teachers that looked like me. The school even sent me to a speech teacher to help me slow down my words. One day she gave me a mirror and told me to look in the mirror when I was trying to speak so I could see myself talking.

I was living in Los Angeles in 1966, every radio was a soundtrack reminding me that I was black, and I was proud (James Brown).

Ms. Echols, when you died, everyone in the black community in Bakersfield knew that someone had killed you and hung you in the shower. The black community feared that their black men would get beat up or hung because back then a black man was beaten and killed for

*Josephine holding hands with mom, Mrs. S with family
in Los Angeles*

talking to, or even looking at, a white woman. Ms. Echols, you were a white woman found dead in a black community. The non-black part of Bakersfield had written you off as white trash and there was nothing lower than white trash. Mr. & Mrs. S were afraid they would lose me because I was never legally adopted, so I understood why they would do anything in their power to protect me and keep me safe. They did not want me to go into Child Protective Services because they were afraid they would never be able to get me out of that system. My birth certificate stated that my mother and father were both white, which was not true but if a baby was to be adopted, it would have a better chance if both parents were white. You were always looking out for your babies and wanted nothing but the best for them.

Ms. Echols, Bakersfield's black community still talked about you. They talked about how you were kind and nice to everyone. They would say things like it was a damn shame how you were treated. It was as though you were a black person that had been shot or killed by the police. Mr. S would often say the only difference between the South and California was that you knew what you were dealing with in the South; in California it was hidden under a badge.

You worked the morning shift at the cafe and the night shift at the bar. No one had reported you missing although everyone had seen you get beat up time and time again. No one came looking for you, so you were found on July 7th. Supposedly someone had called the Sheriff and reported that they heard a white woman screaming for help. Your rap sheet was long, you were fresh out of jail, working at a bar, sleeping with black men, and living in a black community. Some folks said you got what you deserved. They said, "She did it to herself. I would have killed myself

too if I was her."

All the volatile and nasty things that you can imagine came out of the mouths of everyday, regular people. Ms. Echols, you deserved better than going out with the shame that you had taken your own life; the life that you had fought so very hard for, for yourself and for your babies. You weighed about 155 pounds, you were 5' 7, and the shower was 5 feet in that tiny little house. But that's how they found you, hanging in the shower with yellow kitchen curtains around your neck.

Martha, your sister, had just sent you money so that you could move out of the area because she feared for your life. Your sisters would come to lay you to rest - Barbara, Martha, and your twin sister Sally. There was a small graveside service. Martha had pawned a few things for your headstone and with the help from the other sisters, they laid you to rest in Bakersfield's Union Cemetery. The area that was available to you was called Heaven's Rest at Union Cemetery. Mr. D did not come nor did he bring your children. Mr. & Mrs. S did not attend because they were afraid somebody might want to take me away.

Ms. Echols, we moved to Compton, to a little two bedroom house with a patio and a large magnolia tree in the front yard. I got a little puppy too. The school was close by and there was a church on the corner. A lot of things would happen in that little house over the next two years.

One summer, the boy from Bakersfield stayed with us. We fought like cats and dogs, as always, and his two sisters came to Los Angeles with him. One night we went to a bonfire at the Watts festival. We attended a parade earlier that same day. When we got home, the boy and I got into a big fight. He told me that Mr. & Mrs. S had found me in the streets because my own mother did not want me and one day, they would find me hanging from shower too because I was white trash just like my mother. He said "Go tell you little crybaby, I don't care, go tell." Well, I ran to get Mrs. S but I did not find her right away, so I ran throughout the house searching for her. One of his sisters stopped me and asked, "What's wrong with you, why are you running through the house?" With big tears in my eyes, I asked her where Mrs. S was and she said she had gone to the store but would be right back. She asked me what was wrong. "Why are you crying?" she said. I told her what the boy had said to me and the look on her face was very strange.

I knew at that very moment most of what he had said was true. She called her sister over and repeated everything I had said to her and they both made strange faces. One of

Miss Watts 1967

the sisters said, "When Mrs. S gets back, please don't tell her what the boy told you. It would upset her and make her sad.

And please, whatever you do, do not tell Mr. S what the boy said to you." Then one of the sisters called someone on the phone and a few minutes later the boy was picked up from our little house and sent to another house close by that belonged to a family member. They kept saying, "Remember this will be our little secret, so please do not tell Mr. S or Mrs. S. You like hanging out with us, don't you? Going to the park and the bonfire. Didn't you have fun today at the parade?" Then they put some music on and said, "Let's see you dance." By the time Mrs. S got home, I was just dancing around the house having a good time.

I would later meet Sally and her baby girl. We had gone to their apartment and helped them pack everything up. They were going to come and live with us for a while. I was so happy; I just loved the baby and I had someone to play with. Sally's baby could walk a little and she was so beautiful to me. When Sally would go to work at night as a nurse, the baby would sleep in my room with me in the other twin bed.

Her legs would hang down to my knees. She was like a real, life-size baby doll and cute as a button. She needed someone to take care of her and look out for her but I'm not sure I was the right choice. One day I dragged her on my hip outside with me to play in the car just to listen to the radio so we could sing really loud along with the songs. My real, life-size baby doll always smiled at me. She would nod her head up and down, which meant yes, and side to side, which meant no. I was in the driver's seat, and she was in the passenger seat, until the car started rolling back out of the driveway. I had to grab her and jump out of the car. I was 7 years old but in my mind, I was grown!

Sally was fun to talk to and she would listen to me go on and on. It was strange that Sally looked just like you, Ms. Echols. I would find myself always staring at her but there was something about her that was very different from you. It did not matter to me though. The thing is no one ever said this is Ms. Echols's sister Sally, I just knew deep down inside of me that she was related to you. Later on, I would meet Martha, or should I say Jean. Jean was how I was introduced to her. She was Sally's sister and a movie star in Hollywood. Or, at least in my mind, I thought that she was a big Hollywood star. One day Sally, her baby and I were picked up by Jean to spend the day with her. It was a field trip for me. I never went anywhere without Mr. or Mrs. S and I wanted to go even when Mrs. S was trying to convince me not to. She did not have a reason for me not to go and Mr. S had already said I could go. That's what I kept saying to Mrs. S over and over again.

By then, I called Mr. S Daddy and Mrs. S Momma. They were the only parents I knew – they were my momma and daddy and I was their little girl. I was told that Sally and the Baby Doll were just good friends but I had a preconceived sense deep in my soul, Ms. Echols. I just loved them. This caused a jealousy where Mrs. S felt that I favored them because they were white women, that I would not love her more because she was a black woman. That was not true.

After our day together in the Hollywood Hills, Sally and her baby quickly moved out. I was so sad; I did not want them to go. Mr. & Mrs. S were fighting all the time and their fights always seemed to be about Sally. Mrs. S felt that she was being treated like a maid. Sally worked nights, woke up at noon, and would leave with the baby and not come back until it was time for her shift. Although Sally gave them money to help out, this arrangement had to end sooner or later.

The "movie star" Jean gave me her phone number, and I would call her just to say "Hi." The fighting between Mr. & Mrs. S continued even after Sally and my beautiful life-sized Baby Doll were gone. I remember Mrs. S and I were in a car accident. When we got home, several people came over to check on us. Mr. S had been drinking a lot and he was very upset. He walked into the bedroom, got his .22 caliber pearl-handled revolver, came back into the living room, and shot up in the air.

Everyone got up, ran out of the house, and left. He said to Mrs. S, "The next one is going straight through your cold, black heart." He walked towards her and started beating her with the gun. I ran over to him, grabbing his arm, crying for him to stop. I said "What's going to happen to me if you kill her?" He looked at me and stopped. I grabbed Mrs. S by the arm and ran her to the bathroom. She had blood running down her face, so I turned on the tub faucet, and told her to put her head under the water. I saw her brains in the tub! I ran across the street to our neighbor's house crying and screaming, "He killed her, he killed her, I saw her brains!"

A neighbor's wife ran across the street and drove Mrs. S to the hospital. The man let me in his house and the girl tried to comfort me. I could not stop shaking and my stuttering came back. Our neighbors, across the street, had two children, a boy and a girl. The girl and I were close in age and the boy was a little older. The parent's would let me come over from time to time to play with the girl, but she was never allowed to come to my house. They turned on the television for me and I just sat there looking at the screen through my tears. Some kind of moaning sound was coming out of me, like a wounded animal caught in a trap.

There was a big bang at the front door; Mr. S had come for me. He was banging on the door with his shotgun and said that if I didn't come out, he would come in. The neighbor opened the door and the girl told me I had to go with him or he might kill her family. I walked out across the street with Mr. S. Blood was everywhere in the house. It looked like a combat zone with bullet holes through the walls and the ceiling. He sat on the couch with one eye open and one eye closed and both guns next to him. He told me to clean up, so I cleaned the living room and the bathroom the best I could.

The entire time, I thought Mrs. S was dead and was never coming back. When I went into their bedroom, all of her clothes were ripped up and scattered all over the floor. I walked back into the living room and saw that Mr. S was asleep. I tiptoed over to him, took the shotgun and hid it under the bed in my room. I tiptoed back and took the small gun and hid it in the bathroom. Then, I sat down on the floor in a corner of the living room holding back my tears. If this part of my life was a movie, this scene would have Melissa Manchester's "Don't Cry Out Loud" (1978) playing. These lyrics became a soundtrack for my life:

DON'T CRY OUT LOUD, JUST KEEP IT INSIDE
AND LEARN HOW TO HIDE YOUR FEELINGS

Mr. S woke up and called out to Mrs. S. I told him she was not home yet and that she was still at the hospital, if she's not already dead. I got off the floor and walked over to him. I sat in his lap and laid my head on his chest and told him everything was going to be okay. I heard a car drive up and a door open and close. I thought it was the police here to arrest Mr. S. The front door opened slowly and Mrs. S came in with one eye blackened and a big, white head wrap. She just smiled at me. Trying not to wake him, I very carefully got up from Mr. S's lap and we tiptoed into the bedroom and held each other. The next day Mr. S took us to a cafe for breakfast. We would never go out to eat so it was a big deal. He kept saying how sorry he was and that he did not mean to hurt her, but she made him do it.

The next time I called Jean on the phone I said more than just "Hi." I wanted her to come and get me; I wanted to spend the day with her again. She asked me if I would like to spend the weekend with her. She could pick me up Friday afternoon and bring me back Sunday afternoon. I told her, "Yes!" It was the middle of the week and I could not wait for Friday. Even the girl across the street was happy for me and she let me borrow her small suitcase. Mr. S was happy for me too and, because it was up to him if I stayed or went, he said yes, have fun. That Friday morning Mrs. S told me that I did not have to go school because she did not feel well. I tried everything to cheer her up. We played cards, we drank beer, we played dominos but nothing worked. She was sad and not at all happy for me that I was going with Jean.

Mrs. S told me that if I went with Jean, that "white woman" was not going to bring me back and she would never see me again. She said that's why she had been crying all day and that's why she did not feel good. Mrs. S said that I needed to call Jean right away and tell her not to come pick me up. I could tell her I changed my mind.

"You do still love me don't you?" She questioned me. "I have been a good momma to you, why are you hurting me like this, why are you breaking my heart?" I just kept looking at her asking why, I didn't understand why I could not go. I said, "I do love you momma, I do love you." Then she said, "No you don't, you don't love me, you love that white woman! If you loved me you would not go with her." She handed me the phone and said, "Prove it to me, prove that you love me, call her and tell her you've changed your mind." With tears rolling down my face, I picked up the phone and dialed the number but there was no answer.

Jean The Movie Star

A few hours later, Jean was at the door to pick me up. I was told to go to my room and not to come out. I stood there listening as they talked at the front door. Jean did not come inside the house and Mrs. S told her I was sick, maybe another time. She said, "You know how kids are, they say one thing and do another; they can never make up their own minds. I told her to call you this morning. I thought she had called you and told you not to come but she is taking a nap right now. Maybe another time would be better. Mr. S did not really want her to go anyway. I don't want any trouble with him about you coming to try and take her away from me."

Jean just stood there looking around the inside of the house in disbelief. I wanted to come running out and say, "She is lying, she is lying, I DO want to go with you!"

In 1968, I walked home from school, as always. Mrs. S was sitting in front of the television crying. She called someone one the phone and said, "Did you see on TV that they killed him?! They killed Martin Luther King Jr.!" The next few days were tense in our country and in our household as well. Mr. S kept telling me to stay away from the window and stop looking out of it all the time. I could not go out in the front yard or climb the magnolia tree. I had to play in the backyard until 6:00 p.m. and then come inside. The sun was still out, but Mr. S said there was a curfew and people had to be inside by 6:00 p.m. There were several days when I could not go to school because the school was closed and the streets were on fire. I had never seen streets on fire and that is why I wanted to look out the window. The killing of Dr. Martin Luther King Jr. had people upset and most were afraid.

Los Angeles Riots ~1968

Los Angeles Riots airal view

I Said I Wasn't
Going to Tell Nobody

I hated leaving Los Angeles, but it wasn't long before we moved back to Bakersfield. My life would change forever – I had to grow up really fast. Mr. S had bought a horse. I loved horses and had always wanted one. The horse was big, and his name was "Goboy." The man who sold Mr. S the horse told him to make sure that little girl (meaning me) did not ride him by herself. Mr. S rode the horse in the Black History Parade and won awards. We lived in a tiny house and the horse was kept in the backyard. "Goboy" was a Morgan stallion, black with a white spot in the middle of his forehead and his feet were white as though he had white socks on. I fed him, gave him sugar cubes, and spent a lot of time talking to him, affectionately gazing into his big brown eyes. Mr. S would leave for work early, about 4:00 a.m. and in the summertime, around 6:00 a.m. I would get up and go outside to talk to "Goboy."

One morning, I decided I was going to ride him! Mr. S had rigged the little gate, so if anyone tried to take the horse out, he would know. To avoid getting caught in the booby trap, I thought it wise to bring the horse through the house! "Goboy" and I went into the house through the back door, I walked him through the kitchen, the living room, and out the front door. Painstakingly, I dragged the saddle outside, placed it on one chair then stood on the other chair to reach the horse's back. After getting the saddle on and pulling it as hard as I could, I still had to use the chair to get onto the horse.

I rode around the front yard sliding from side-to-side because the saddle needed to be tightened.

A young man, walking up the street, caught my attention. I said, "Hey mister! Can you help me with this saddle?" The man looked at me like I was crazy or maybe he was just afraid of the horse. He slowly walked into the yard and said to me, "Little girl, do you know what you're doing?" I said, "Yes sir. I do this all the time. I'm just having a little trouble with the saddle." The man tightened the saddle and before he could leave the yard, Goboy and I were off and running! He knew how to go right, he knew how to go left. He would listen to me, we slowed down when I thought I would fall off. I felt free!

We rode to the corner store and grown men appeared afraid of the horse. They were yelling at me to get off the horse before I got hurt. I just laughed at them and took off to the nearest open field. I was free as long as I got the horse home before Mr. S came back from work. We headed home and the horse knew the way. I hurried to put him up but Goboy had this white foam all over his back. I gave him lots of water, brushed his back, and fed him so that I could tell Mr. S I had already fed the horse today and he would have no reason to check on his horse.

That was the best day of my childhood and freedom felt good. In my mind, I was 9 going on 30.

In a few short years, in what seemed to happen overnight, I became a young woman. That particular morning, I asked Mrs. S if I could stay home from school. It was Friday, the last day of school, I had a decent year: I was my middle school's president. I played softball, and I was a member of the Glee Club. I was always sore from horse riding but the night before, I had stayed up with stomach aches. Staying home also meant that I would not have to hear Cher's song on the radio, "Half-Breed. It was like clockwork. Every morning, on the way to school, the song would come on the bus. The kids would sing the song and look at me. They would change the lyrics to say, "All you'll ever be is half mutt."

I excused myself to the restroom; when I wiped, there was blood everywhere. I thought I was dying. Why is God killing me? What had I done? I said my prayers every night. I called Mrs. S and she came to the door and said, "What's the matter with you now?" I said, "Mom (Mr. and Mrs. S were the only parents I knew), "I don't know, I think God is killing me; there is blood everywhere!" She laughed and said, "Wait here I'll be right back." It felt like an eternity. She returned from the store with a brown paper bag that she gave to me. Inside, there was a sanitation pad with two safety pins. She said, "Don't stick yourself !" No instructions on what to do; no explanations on what was happening to me. I went to my room and Mrs. S came in and said, "Wait till I tell Mr. S." I begged and pleaded with her not to.

That evening, Mr. S, parked his truck in the driveway, before he could get to the house, Mrs. S was there to greet him. She told him, "Our fast little girl started her period today." What was a period? What did I do to upset God so much He decided to kill me? Mr. S called me from the living room and his tone indicated that I was in some kind of trouble. I walked into the living room and stood looking at him and her and he said, "Is it true? Is it true you got your rag?" I just stood there not knowing what to say, then he began to yell at me just like he yelled at Mrs. S before she was beaten. I was turning around to go to my room, and from nowhere, he grabbed me and began beating me with a broom. He was yelling at me that I was just like my dead momma, I was a whore and would never be anything but a whore, just like Ms. Echols.

During the beating, I began to ask myself questions. What was a "whore?" Did he just say white woman, Ms. Echols, is my mother? When the broom broke, he stopped. Blood was everywhere. I couldn't even cry anymore. Like a wounded animal I crawled to my room. I was shaking, moaning, very confused, and in a great amount of pain. I could hear Mr. & Mrs. S fighting but I didn't care anymore. I shut my door, put a pillow over my head, and eventually I fell asleep. I stayed inside of my room the entire weekend. I cut up the pillow case to use for pads. I would tiptoe out to use the restroom, then quickly hurry back to my room. In my mind, I was 11 years old, still going on 30 because time stood still since moving to Bakersfield; God was killing me because I was a whore with a rag.

Monday came, I was a little black and blue, still in pain. A neighbor lady, who lived a few houses over from us, stopped by to ask if she could use the phone. When she saw me, she asked if it would be okay if I went to church with her family. Her church was having a program for children all that week. Before Mrs. S could say anything I said, "Yes, yes I would like to go." She said they would pick me up around 5:00 p.m. and bring me back about 8:00 p.m. The car drove up, they blew the horn and I came out. They had a daughter about my age and a son close to my age. I knew the girl from school and sometimes we would walk home together. The neighbor lady was pregnant with a child and had another little baby in her arms. I had been to church before when we lived in Compton. The Compton church was big and pink and located on the corner near our house.

At the Compton church there was lots of singing, dancing and shouting and the people seemed really happy. It also had a vacation Bible study program that I sometimes attended. The neighbor lady's church in Bakersfield was small.

I was always searching for God and I felt good when the preacher started to preach. I would look right into his eyes. At the end of the night he asked if anyone wanted to come to the Lord as they were baptizing people who came up. It felt good to my soul, I went back every night. All of the kids had been baptized.

It was the last night of Summer Revival, when I thought about whether or not I would go up at the end of the sermon.

On this night, I was holding the baby and before the preacher started to preach, he asked if someone else could hold the baby. I did not understand, maybe I did something wrong, but I just loved holding the baby. The neighbor lady who drove me to church took her baby and smiled at me and said, "It's okay, God loves you." The preacher finished preaching and then he looked right at me and said, "Do you want to come up here and accept the Lord Jesus into your heart?" I looked up at him and said, "Yes." The whole church was very happy; everyone started singing and dancing.

My neighbor, the lady with the baby, held my hand and walked me up to this little room where I put on a white gown and then she led me up to the baptism pool. What they did not know; I couldn't swim and had a fear of drowning.

The church people continued singing and praying. I stepped into the pool and the preacher said to me, "Repeat after me: Romans 10:9 'That if thou shalt confess with thy mouth the Lord Jesus, and shalt believe in thine heart that God hath raised him from the dead, thou shalt be saved.'" I repeated it. Then he asked me, "Do you confess it out of your mouth?" and I said, "Yes." He asked, "Do you believe it, in your heart, that He was raised from the dead?" I said, "Yes." Then he told me to hold my nose and he rubbed oil on my head. Down I went into the water, and up I came, and down I went, and up I came. As I was going down again he said, "I baptize you in the name of the Father, the Son and the Holy Ghost."

The people were all around when I came up for the last time. The neighbor lady with the baby came up to me and led me back to the room so that I could change back into my clothes. I started moving all around and I was saying over and over, Thank you Jesus! Thank you Jesus!

My baptism was an outward expression, not only symbolism, for me. As if, I was taking off old clothes and putting on new ones, even though I wasn't. I felt new and began to speak a new language. Church people call it speaking in Tongues. I felt good in my heart and all over on the inside. I was happy, overjoyed with unspeakable joy! It was like a ball of fire down on the inside of my soul, yet it was peaceful and I was saved, a child of God! My name was written in the Lambs Book of Life, I was 11 years old and can still remember it like it was yesterday. I will never forget the song they were singing that night:
I said I wasn't going to tell nobody (but I)
Couldn't keep it to myself (no, I)
Couldn't keep it to myself (no, I)
Couldn't keep it to myself

What the Lord has done for me!
You oughta been there (You oughta been there)
When He Saved my soul!

One thing the preacher said to me before we left was that he wanted me to fast for three days. He said it would make me strong in the Lord. I asked him, "What do you mean, what is fast?" He said the neighbor lady would explain it to me on the ride home. He gave me a Bible and told me to start with the Book of Matthew and read the Bible every day.

We drove back home and they dropped me off. Mrs. S opened the door. She gave me a hug and said, "Why is your hair wet?" I told her I had been baptized, accepted the Lord as Jesus Christ, that the Holy Ghost came upon me and I spoke in tongues. She said, "Good for you, now go to bed, I'll talk to you tomorrow. On the ride home, the neighbor lady explained that when we fast we don't eat anything until the sun goes down. She said, "I know it's going to be hard and the first day is always the hardest." Then she asked me if God gave me a song down in my heart and I said, "Yes." She told me to keep praying, read the word of God every day, hold the song in my heart and go to church with them on Sundays. God was not killing me but saving me. He even replaced Cher's song with a new song. I said I wasn't going to tell anybody what the Lord had done for me.

Ms. Echols, I felt so very happy and stayed on the fast for three days. The 4th of July was around the corner and Mr. & Mrs. S and I were going over to celebrate at their friend's house. I was looking forward to it. Maybe they would have fireworks and there would be kids for me to play with.

A few days before the 4th of July, Mr. S came home drunk. I sat in the living room reading my Bible and he started in on me. He said, "You think you are a Holy roller? You think you are better than me?" He took the Bible from me and threw it out the door. Mr. S said, "Can't nothing save you." I just sat there waiting for a beating to come. Instead he just walked away. I went to bed angry with him and when I said my prayers, I did not ask God to bless him. I just layed there in bed thinking to myself that I had to leave this house.

I had tried leaving more than once; I was labeled as a "runaway" and had even spent 10 days in juvenile because of it. I did not know that day would be the day because I didn't plan for it, it just happened. Mrs. S had given me $20 to go to the corner store for her. She said, "bring back my change." The city bus had just started a route in our community. It just so happened to be pulling up to the store as I was walking up. I got on the bus. It was air-conditioned (Bakersfield is known for Summer temperatures peaking over 110 degrees!) I could sit while it drove me around town and brought me back. No big deal.

The bus was passing a nearby park. I noticed some older kids I knew sitting under a tree. They looked like they were having fun! I pulled the cord to stop the bus, got out, walked over to the group, and sat on the grass. The kids were talking about the fair that was coming in September. They were saying this year it was going to be good because Cool and the Gang and Chaka Khan were performing. The kids were drinking and smoking.

I had smoked cigarettes but I didn't really like to drink. Alcohol did not make me feel good. The smell reminded me of Mr. S. He could be nice but when he drank, he was mean. The older kids were smoking weed. I had seen it but had never smoked it. I did not want to seem like a baby when someone passed a joint around and it came to me. I hit the joint two times. Puff, puff, pass. It came around again, but as I reached for it, everything became fuzzy. The kids laughed and said, "She's high already." I wanted to go home because I knew I should get back before Mr. S returned home from work. I offered one kid five dollars to drive me home.

Already high, I could barely get in the car and as I laid down on the back seat, my head was spinning and I felt sick. Just as we were about to turn the corner to my house, I lifted up my head from the back seat and saw Mr. S's truck in front of us ready to pull into our driveway. It was too late. If he saw me like this, I would not be able to avoid a beating. I pleaded with the boy to keep driving. I told him I would give him money to take me anywhere but home. He said he was from Los Angeles and had come up to visit some folks. His plan was to go home in the morning. He offered to let me come with him to a hotel to chill for the night. I agreed. I was still getting high by sitting in the car full of smoke. I don't remember going to his room. It was like I was conscious but I wasn't. (Later, I discovered the joints were "wet". I was not only high from weed.) The lights were on but I was far from home. I remembered it was still daytime when I was in the car but when I realized where I was, it was dark outside and I was alone in the hotel room.

I was naked. All of the lights were off, except in the bathroom. I got up and went toward the light and took a cold shower for a long, long time.

There was no way I could go home; somebody would probably end up hurt or dead and that somebody would probably be me. I was not going back to juvenile hall. Yes, I had messed up, big time. Then I remembered a young man who worked at the Greyhound Bus Station, a young man who had pawed over me. If I could make it there, maybe he would help me buy a ticket to Los Angeles. It was about 3:00 a.m. and he had told me he worked the night shift. When I opened the motel door, I saw lots of trucks in the parking lot and a cafe.

I remembered that the city bus had come this way early in the day, so if I started walking towards downtown, I would end up at the bus station. I talked with the young man who worked at the Greyhound Bus Station. He put me on a bus to Los Angeles that morning around 6:00 a.m. He bought me a round trip ticket and also gave me $50. I slept the whole trip and when I woke up in downtown Los Angeles, What am I going to do now? There was no turning back! I got off the bus, went into the restroom and washed up. Inside the bus station, I bought something to eat and a newspaper, then sat down and started looking for a job. When the first person that walked up to me asked me my name, I lied to them. This is when I started living a lie that lasted for many years. Being a runaway was a crime, so I could not use my real name. I was fresh meat in a game called life.

At 11-years old, I not only called myself, I became Shelly Wright.

It is a cold, dog-eat-dog world where everyone and everything was fake, until shit got real.

SAVED BY HIS *Amazing Grace*

Josephine's School picture at ten years

Things got real one moment, hanging out with a group of familiar male friends had taken me out with them. They were playing cards and everyone was having a good time. A roar of yells emerged, hollering, and laughter. I had gotten second-hand laughter and was smiling when one of the familiar faces caught my attention.

He had a serious face and asked me, "What are you laughing for? We were betting for YOU!" I felt the realization in the pit of my stomach. At age 11, I was sold in a game of poker.

As of today, 2022, "an estimated 200,000 American children at risk for trafficking into the sex industry."
(U.S. Department of Justice. ncjrs.gov)

Shelly Wright

At first, I stayed on Skid Row at a motel for $5. It was a room with a bed, one sheet, one kitchen chair and the bathroom was down the long hallway. The lock on the door was broken, the small window was broken, and the lights were dim. A young man I met at the bus station showed me where the place was. The kind of young men who hang around bus stations prey on the naivety of the most vulnerable in our society.

This young man could tell I was afraid. Saying that you are 24 years old and acting like you are 24 years old are two different things. He could probably smell my bullshit but if I was selling it, he knew just how to make me feel safe. He offered to stay and watch the broken door and of course I accepted the offer.

I spent nights out sleeping in the park downtown in Los Angeles just wandering up and down the streets. During the day, I would get free cigarettes from people handing out samples of Newports and Kools. Sitting down at a table after people got up and walked away, in order to eat. Funny thing is, one day you are on the inside looking out and trying to get out, then you find yourself on the outside looking in. I did get a job as a waitress but never got paid. I was able to hang out in the movie theater all day and all night and eat popcorn, soda and candy. Nobody ever asked what a child was doing out here. Yes, adults know the difference between a child and an adult.

Ms. Echols, it did not take long, I was 13 and pregnant. I had my own apartment and my baby's father had no clue who I was, Josephine, 13. He believed I was Shelly Wright, 24. The same age he was. The lie. In the beginning, we were happy. We had been together a year or so. By then, I knew how to act like I was 24." He was nice to me and I thought I was in love. His sister and I worked together at a massage parlor. She had a pimp and I had a boyfriend; it was her brother who worked at a gas station. We were both green when it came to the street game so we held on to each other for as long as we could until I became pregnant.

I was about seven months pregnant and shit was getting too real. The fast nightlife was not working so well anymore. The last time I saw him we were fighting about the other woman and, from his point of view, somebody had to make money because I could not work. That's when I blew up and told the stable of girls to go home, by encouraging them to go to their homes. Saying, "Get off the streets! Stop selling your bodies for someone who could never love you for who you are! They are just using you to make money for themselves. Go home! Try to work things out a different way before you end up dead, out on the streets!"

I had been beaten, raped, sold, and traded in a three-card molly game. I know it was God's grace and mercy that kept me from getting into drugs or losing my mind. I guess I was preaching to myself because no one else listened. That's when I said to my baby's father, "You don't know anything about me. You don't even know my real name."

Most people on the street or in "the life" don't use their real names anyway, but when I told him how old I was that's when he lost it. I ended up at the bottom of the stairs and I never saw my baby's father again. I tried to contact him a few times but the conversation was always the same. He needed money and he wanted me to come back and go to work for him. Ms. Echols, that's when I returned home to Bakersfield.

Mr. S was no longer drinking and things seemed like they might work out. One day there was a knock at the door and there stood a nicely-dressed black lady. I thought she was a friend of Mrs. S from her church but she happened to be my Probation Officer (P.O.). I didn't even know I had a P.O. Away we went to juvenile hall because I was still considered a runaway. I had to stay another ten days in juvenile hall before they let me come home.

Ms. Echols, it was now September. I had turned 14 and was giving birth to Diamond, after 21 hours of labor. I thought for sure I was going to die. I kept asking them to cut me open and take the baby out! The nurse only assured me this baby is coming out the same way it got in there.

God is amazing. As soon as she was born and the afterbirth came out, they handed her to me and the pain was gone. She was beautiful! I counted ten toes and ten fingers and she was mine. Ms. Echols, it was at that moment that I said to myself, "My momma did not owe me anything; she gave me life and the rest was left up to me." I had always felt your presence. I can only explain what I mean by that by saying it feels like the essence of you was in me from the last time I saw you, when we laughed together, eating potato peels and ice-cream. The long hug imparted something in me, it hid the best parts of you inside of me."

Los Angeles Bus Terminal

The P.O. sent me to group sessions and sometimes we would do things like bowling. One afternoon with the group, she talked to me and asked me, "What are you going to do?" I said, "Maybe I'll be a writer" and she laughed and said, "Maybe a maid." Then she said, "You know we just finished building a brand new juvenile hall for fast girls like you down in the Los Angeles area. So, you had better not give me any problems because we have a place for bad girls like you. You will be 21 before you ever get out of that place." The one thing that the streets taught me was to listen to what was not being said. I was thinking this black lady was my friend, that she was going to look out for a young Sister and maybe I could even be like her. But no, just like so many people in power, they can't share goodness because they act out of fear that they might not have a job if the problem was ever really fixed.

Mr. S & Mrs. S were fighting again. It was just a matter of time before I was in the middle. Now, all he had to do was pick up the phone and call my P.O. and I would be gone for seven years. This was the first and only time I thought about killing myself because I could not leave and take my baby with me and I could not stay. I asked if I could become emancipated. Yes, that was laughed at too. How was I supposed to be a 14-year-old child when I had already lived a 24-year-old grown woman's life?

After Mr. & Mrs. S had a big fight, Mr. S said, "I am calling her P.O. tomorrow and we can keep the baby." I knew I had to go. That morning, before Mr. S went to work, he told Mrs. S to Call and tell my P.O. to meet him at home after he got off from work. After he left, I went to Mrs. S and said to her," I am leaving and I am not taking my baby. I know you will take good care of her for me, but I need you to understand something: I am not going to die like my mother Ms. Echols did, and I am coming back for her when I turn 18. All I need is a head start" I hugged my six-month baby girl and told her I had to leave. I know she didn't understand, but I wanted her to know that I loved her with all my heart and soul and I would be back for her. As I walked towards the door, she began to cry and I ran back, picked her up, and started singing to her, *"Hush little baby don't you cry mama's gonna buy you a mockingbird."* Then I handed her to Mrs. S and walked out the front door.

I went back to the Greyhound Bus Station and headed North. I knew they would be looking for me in Los Angeles. I went to Fresno. A young man was traveling with me and it was puppy love. He got a job as a busboy and I got a job as a maid and we were able to stay at the hotel where I worked. I called back to Bakersfield and the person I spoke with said my baby was okay but the young man's mother did not understand why her son left as they did not have any problems at home-like I did.

One night, when he got off from work I told him I had a bus ticket for him to go back home. I knew that eventually he would resent me because he would miss his mother. I asked him to do me a favor and call me if he was forced to tell them where I was. He did call me and said he was picked up at the bus station before he was able to get home. The authorities had caught him and made him tell them where I was living. I understood and thanked him for his kindness and for calling me.

Tracy Brooks

Ms. Echols, this is when I became Tracy Brooks. I was gone before the Sun came up; getting rides in big-wheeled trucks and on the backs of motorcycles. I ended up in Compton, CA, living with whomever would open their door for a night or two. I got a job at IHOP. I was a decent waitress. Friends would let me sleep on their couches a little longer, when I had an income.

The restaurant hired a new manager, he gave me more hours and I could work on Sundays (customers tipped more on Sundays). There was an instance when the manager asked me to bring him coffee. As a good waitress, I asked how he liked it. He replied, "Like you."

Ms. Echols, I was almost 15 years old when I moved in with him. He thought I was Tracy Brooks, 24 years old. Back then, we were paid in cash. You did not need identification, there wasn't a pay stub, and you kept all of your tips. He was almost 20 years older than me. I was young, dumb, and full of hope. He was the first man to ask me to stay after spending a night with him. He was nice to me. Kindness was a much-needed relief from running around while carrying a weight in my heart. We would go out dancing-I loved to dance! I could not work at the IHOP any more because he was the manager. It felt good to play Housewife. He became my Old Man.

After moving in, it took very little time for me to become pregnant again. I was afraid. To my surprise, when I told The Old Man that I was 15 and pregnant with his child, he was happy and assured me that it was going to be ok. That's when he told me, "You can never tell anybody who you are or how old you really are." I felt safe because he didn't lose his mind like my baby girl's father did. Then, he lost his job. I never knew why. We quickly lost our place. When I was about seven months pregnant, we moved into a hotel in downtown Los Angeles. We had just enough money between us for me to take a round-trip bus to ride to North Hollywood to see my doctor and come back.

There was one day that I will never forget. I was sitting at a bus stop, waiting for my route to take me home from my prenatal checkup. I met a woman named Susan. Our meeting began when she asked if I could break her bill of cash into change. "No," I replied. She walked away and came back in time to catch the bus. Susan sat right beside me. She asked me all sorts of questions: How old are you? Is there a father? Do you have any family? Do you have food? I was not in the mood.

My thoughts were solely on what we were going to do the next day; the rent was overdue and we would be evicted from the hotel. The bus had come to a stop and I had to transfer buses. Susan was gone. Suddenly, she returned.

"Here's my number," she said. "Call me if you need anything." Yeah, right, lady! Have a nice day. I kept my thoughts to myself and placed her number in my coat's pocket.

The following morning, I went to the hotel's lobby to check the phone booths for change. I found $2.25! As I put the money into my pocket, I felt the piece of paper with Susan's number on it. I was curious as to why she handed it to me. I weighed the risk of a quarter to get the answer. I called her. Susan asked where I was, I told her.

As we spoke on the phone, her husband, James, appeared in the hotel. He paid the outstanding hotel rent and a few days more. James gave me food and promised to come back. He did. James came back and spent time driving me around town to find an apartment. We found one. James and Susan paid three month's rent and then, they disappeared.

I turned 16. My sweet, Leo, was born. I always told him the story about how God sent his angels, James and Susan, to help us.

Time passed. Now, as a family, we left the Greater Los Angeles area and moved to San Francisco. There is no place like The City of San Francisco. We were there for just a small amount of time before we moved to Vallejo, California. The thought of my baby girl baby girl weighed heavily on my mind. I called her, occasionally. I would even visit (when Mr. S was out of town), so that my baby girl would know who I was. It was not easy but life was never easy for me. My son, Leo, was my "Cookie Monster," always grinning and making me smile. He was my "Man Child" and our bond was strong.

In the Summer of 1979, I turned 18. This was the perfect time for me to ask Mrs. S if I could come get my baby. Getting custody of Diamond became my main focus.

Mrs. S had to travel out of state to attend a funeral. My little girl, now 4, would stay in Bakersfield. I proposed to pick up my daughter at the end of August, while Mrs. S was away. She agreed.

When I arrived in Bakersfield, I stopped by a relative's house. I told them I was there to get my baby girl. They had already heard about me coming down but told me that Mr. S would not let me have my baby back. There was a rumor going around: if I showed up, Mr. S was going to kill me! He had taken my baby into hiding elsewhere-I knew exactly where she was.

I went to the Bakersfield Police Station, they redirected me to the Kern County Sheriff's Department. I explained to them that I was in Bakersfield to pick up my daughter and that Mr. S refused to give me my child.

Their response was that there was nothing they could do. I said, "Fine. I understand… But I want you to know that I am going to get my child back. You can either escort me there now or you can meet me there later–one way or another, I AM GOING TO GET MY BABY!"

The person that I was addressing directly notified me that I had a warrant out for my arrest. I was not surprised, "for being a runaway?" My frustrations accumulated as another, cold voice entered the room. "I remember you," the sheriff's officer said. "There's always domestic calls for your house. What do you want from us?" I demanded that I needed their assistance to get my child back. I explained how Mr. S threatened my life, if I went there. I would be a fool to walk into his trap. I repeated, "I just want my baby."

I made statements about when young girls have babies and leave them with someone else, the mother doesn't usually return for the child; I was only going there for her. I made it clear that I didn't have a choice when I left and made sure that they knew I was 18 now and I was going with or without their help.

The Deputy Sheriff decided to go with me but Diamond was not there. Mr. S had all five of his shotguns loaded and was waiting for me. While Law Enforcement tried to talk with him, another unit went to a relative's house where my baby was being hid. The woman there told them that I had abandoned the child. It was a mess! The officers picked up my daughter; unfortunately, they did not bring her to me. Instead, she was taken to "baby jail" and I was told that I would have to go before a judge to get her.

I asked to speak with someone from the Department of Child Services. A young lady, not much older than me, came in-a social worker. She explained to me that my child would stay in their custody until a judge could hear the case. She did not know when that would be. As we talked, I pleaded with the young lady, "Please, help me." I asked, "Do you know any other young girls who had come back for their babies?" I needed her to see this situation from my perspective. I asked if she had any children. "No," she answered. I asked if her mother was alive. "Yes." I begged her, "Then call your mother and ask her what you should do!"

Ms. Echols, of the three men who could have been my father, I contacted the one who was married and had four children. I called to ask him to please tell Child Services that I had not abandoned my child. He told me that he would like to help but couldn't. I was devastated and expressed it, "I bet that's exactly what you told my mother, Ms. Echols," and hung up the phone. His wife called me back and told me SHE had spoken with the authorities and told them that I had NOT abandoned my child. It was the truth, that's all I wanted.

The young social worker came back from her visit with my daughter. She said, "Yes, Diamond does know who you are... And, I did speak with my mother. My mother said it is rare that a young girl comes back for their baby. So, we will release her to you." She opened the door, Diamond came running into my arms, and off we went. It was a long drive back but I did not stop until we were far from Bakersfield, out of Kern County. We pulled over, somewhere near Atwater, for a pit stop. I just kept looking at my daughter; she was so beautiful and I had kept my word to her and to myself.

Ms. Echols, I was so very happy, yet still afraid. When fear is instilled in you, you expect it to show up at any moment, even when things go well.

A Mind is a Terrible Thing to Waste

Ms, Echols, my Diamond began going to a Head Start program. I rode the bus with her and went to school three days a week. Soon after, I did the same with Leo. By the time they were in elementary school, I was a classroom aide for each of them on different days.

I was 20 when my third child, Mandela was born; healthy and strong. He was delivered before Midwives could get to us. I decided to have him at home, with Midwives, because my healthcare provider made me uncomfortable. The doctor would make comments like, "You already have two kids, do you think you need another one?" Or, "Maybe you should have your tubes tied." Those words were upsetting, annoying, insulting, and genuinely made me fearful that the doctor would request a tubal ligation without my permission.

Midwives gave me the same sense of security as James and Susan, the angels God sent; they paid my rent, gave me food,treated me with compassion, and ultimately, saw me as a Human. I did not have family or a support system in Vallejo. I could not leave my children to give birth to my baby. Midwives was a solution for me; they helped me deliver my child at home.

The Old Man would take our family on long walks in the Vallejo hills. The waterfront was nice on a hot, sunny day and made trips to visit the library. We would dumpster-dive for books. Education was something that I always wanted for myself and my children.

We were living during a movement for people of color to have equal rights. I remember seeing the campaign posters for the United Negro College Scholarship fund and began to hear their slogan everywhere, "A Mind is a Terrible Thing to Waste but a Wonderful Thing to Invest in." It stuck with me. Education meant knowledge, a key that would open doors. I was a product of the Sixties and believed that Rev. Dr. Martin Luther King Jr. had died for our right to be educated, when our theme song was, *"Say it Loud, I'm Black and I'm Proud!"* ~James Brown

Living on the streets, education was not easily available, only condemnation and misfortune spread (much like today). Coming from the streets, where there were only disadvantaged, small-minded people who never seemed to dream anymore, it was rare to meet someone educated. The Old Man was good at storytelling, not only could he speak and write very well, he was good at lying.

By 1981, I had an unrelenting yearn–I needed to do more with my life. I enrolled into Solano Community College. I did not do well but it did offer me a view of a wider, bigger perspective of the world. There wasn't childcare at the school. Often, I would bring my newborn, Mandela, to class with me.

The Old Man bought a car for us. It was manual and I did not know how to drive a stick-shift. The Old Man seemed not able, or willing, to teach me.

It was just like that morning with GoBoy, I looked out the window as I made up my mind. Today is the day. I am driving that car! I got in and drove to Los Angeles. I always stayed in contact with Jean and she welcomed me to stay with her. I left my daughter and two sons. I called The Old Man, "I know how to drive a stick!"

That taste of freedom for the first time was burning down in my soul. I could only stay for a day but Jean and I made the most of it by catching up with each other. We talked about you, Ms. Echols. I asked her about how Sally was doing. Jean was supportive without passing judgment on me. I could just be myself.

I admired Jean for carrying herself with confidence. She was gorgeous and smart. Our visit gave me strength to go back home and deal with my life as a young mom. Jean accepted me. She loved me, although we did not always see eye-to-eye; she thought of me as being young-minded, child-like, almost condescending. She would compare me to you, Ms. Echols, often–a dreamer, always hoping for the best. You and I were optimistic people living in a pessimistic world.

Ms. Echols, I loved being a mother. My kids were my life. They made me happy and I tried to make them happy. Just like my grandmother, Pearl, we never had much money but I gave my children all of me-my love, my time.

I went back to school and this time, I did well. I completed a few semesters with good grades. It wasn't until the first time I received an "A" on an assignment I thought, I am not dumb! Things may take longer for me to fully understand but I will study hard until I get it. I have determination and perseverance in my favor!

At age 24, I had my fourth child, Azul, at home with a midwife. My daughter arrived on New Year's Day, 1985. My life was about to change; playing "House Wife" for eight years with an older man began to fall apart in the worst way.

It was at the time that I began to think for myself-not the storytelling-after I went to school. The Old Man was losing control over me. When an abuser knows they can no longer manipulate you, no longer have power, and are desperate, they can do the unimaginable.

Ms. Echols, The Old Man and I were on a double-date with my friend, a lady about my age, and her boyfriend. We had a meeting in the ladies room. While in private she said, "You are the oldest, young woman I have ever met." She then asked, "Do you always agree with everything he says?" My instinct felt that something was wrong with our relationship but I did not know what it was. I did not feel for The Old Man the way that he felt for me. It was getting to the point where I cringed every time he touched me.

Farragut elementary school in Vallejo gave me an opportunity to travel to Sacramento. They invited me to be the parent-representative for the school's Title I program (funding for the under-served and impoverished areas). I was very involved in the programs for my children. I felt that it was important to be involved in my children's education, I wanted them to have a future; so, I left for Sacramento, first, and my family would join me later that week. The school paid for my travel and stay. I had never stayed in such a nice hotel before. I was around such educated people. They did not mind that I was not on their socio level; they respected me for seeking to better my life. This was an opportunity to have a seat at the table; I listened

Josephine with her four children
Diamond, Leo, Mandela, and Azul.

learned, and absorbed.

It seemed like an eternity until I was reunited with my babies. My baby girl, Azul, was six months, and my big girl, Diamond, was 10 years old; she seemed to have grown up overnight. There was a certain sadness in her eyes. I thought it was a result of having to take care of her three younger siblings for a few days without me and was drained from it. Even at 10 years old, she was such a major help to me. My family and I returned home from Sacramento, Diamond still had sad eyes.

One evening, as she came down to say, "Good Night," I noticed something that wasn't right. I saw The Old Man looking at my child, in her see-through nightgown, with Man-Eyes–that look I had seen him give towards me. From deep within my soul, I knew something was wrong.

The following day, it was just my kids and I spending the day together, working; we walked door-to-door, delivering phone books in a little red wagon for extra cash. I asked my Diamond if everything was alright. "Yes, Momma," she replied. I said to her, "You know, there is nothing in this world that you cannot tell me. No matter what it is, you can tell me and I will believe you." Her tears began to flow. I hurried all my children back to our house. Diamond and I went into the bathroom.

As I washed her face, I told her, "It's ok. You can tell me." My daughter's reply was, "I don't want to hurt you, Momma. You have been through so much." Tears streamed while she said, "I thought you knew. You know everything." My heart dropped. I asked her how and when. She gave me details that only I would know about The Old Man. It was just like when I begged Mrs. S, my daughter begged me not to tell her father. "Please,don't say anything. He said he would kill you." I held my child. I told her, "not to tell the Old Man!"

Later, The Old Man came home. We all sat at the dinner table and closed our eyes as he said Grace. As he blessed the food, I asked God, What type of demon is this?

That night, my baby girl, my big girl, and I all slept together. I told The Old Man that they were both sick and I fell asleep in the room with them. The next morning, I loaded my children into the car and left. We made it to Los Angeles and stayed with trusted friends, people that I had known for a long time. When I was a kid, we lived next door to them; they were good, kind people. I just needed a place to stay and space to think for a few days.

It was different when it was just me asking for a couch to crash on. Now, I had four children to care for. For the first time in my life, I decided that I wasn't going to run away anymore. I was not leaving with just the clothes on my back, starting all over again.

I worked hard for what little I had. My life had improved and progressed; now, I was going to school and living in affordable housing. If anyone was going to leave, it was him–not me or my kids!

Ms. Echols, a big storm was hitting California, just like a storm had hit my life. My kids and I were heading home to the Bay Area when the rain closed the grapevine. We were able to make it to Gorman, where we stayed overnight. The next day, we made a stop to Bakersfield; we made a stop to see your grave site.

Then I took my children to visit your twin, Sally, and her daughter, The Baby Doll. My life-sized babydoll had grown to be a beautiful young woman, tall, gorgeous, a supermodel with a life of her own. Her mother, Sally, and I had a very close relationship. I understood her and she understood me. Whenever I was feeling down, she would say, "Just look up and smile. Remember: God loves you!" It was just what I needed to hear to heal my soul. I went to see a preacher; I asked him to pray for me. I knew this demon had come to Kill, Steal, and Destroy me by any means necessary.

My kids and I returned to our home in Fairfield, North of the bay.

The Old Man was in complete denial that anything ever happened. He claimed that my daughter made it up. We agreed to go to family therapy. Afterwards, the counselor called to tell me about new laws that mandated reporting the child abuse that was discussed during our session; he wanted to notify me that he reported it to the police department.

I thanked the man for the call, hung up. I told The Old Man. He said that if the police were to come, he would kill us all!

When they arrived, no one answered the door.

The next morning, while I was combing Diamond's hair, I told her, "Some people are going to come to your school and they are going to want to talk to you. I need you to not tell them what you told me. You have to say that you made it up."

I believed him when he said he would kill us all. There were times we would all be in the car, while he was driving, and he would threaten, "What if I just drove us off a bridge and that would be that?"

I would NOT have my children taken from me in any way. He was a good manipulator and had a way of storytelling, you would believe the bullshit coming out of his mouth. He would ask me, "Who will believe you, with your past?" He tried to convince me, "They will put you in a NutHouse; then, I will have your kids, your daughter, too!" He was evil, "She wants to be with me, anyway."

Ms. Enchols, I had a lot of buried bones; there was a graveyard of history and past lives that I did not speak about. I had a new life: I was in college, the president of the Black Student Union, my kids were in good schools; however, my life was built on lies. The Old Man knew it.

I met a lady, a school teacher, and her husband was a police officer. The woman was always offering help by giving me rides from school (I walked most days). She was kind to me and my children. I looked up to her and could trust this woman. I asked if my kids could spend the night at her house. I knew that if anything were to happen to me, she and her husband would know what to do, my kids would be safe. They would make sure that The Old Man would not have them.

The Old Man thought I wanted alone time to be intimate with him. He did not know that I had called his eldest son, who was a few years younger than me, and told him that his father had to go. He sent an airline ticket for The Old Man to go back to the East Coast and live with him.

I told The Old Man that I believed my daughter and he had to leave; I was done running away and starting over. For him, this was the best bet out of a bad situation. Had he not crossed that unforgiving line, I would have stayed forever.

Manipulation can leave impressions on the mind; the mental abuse can last long after the trauma. The mental scars can last longer than physical abuse, if being beaten doesn't kill you. The black eyes and bruises on the inside of the heart are invisible. We were alone and I did not have to worry about the safety of my kids. If he killed me, so be it. At least my kids would not be harmed.

Our alone time subsequently led to intercourse. For me, sex was lying there with my eyes closed, counting 60 seconds, or until he was done. This time, he began choking me. I was passing out of consciousness. I thought of You, Ms. Echols, This must be what it was like when you died.

Something evil possessed The Old Man and it was like he turned into a dragon on top of me. A big puff of green smoke came out of his mouth as he exhaled. He rolled off of me and began crying like a little worm.

I got up and told him to pack whatever he thought was his. We waited for the Sun to come up. I got my kids and drove him straight to the airport and watched as he boarded the plane. My kids and I walked out of the airport and did not look back. Leo, my oldest son, was at the age of 8. He was upset because he and The Old Man were very close. My baby boy, Mandela, was 5, with a black eye and bruised soul, was happy. He ran and did cartwheels while yelling, "He's gone! He is gone!" My baby girl, Azul, was unaware of this life-changing event, she was only one years old.

Ms. Echols, I did try leaving him before Azul was born. I had gone to a women's shelter, something that was not available to you. Shelters for women who had suffered Domestic Violence were now being advertised on billboards and posters. They were in the places that had said, A Mind is a Terrible Thing to Waste.

I stayed busy as a single mother with four children: I was going to school, working part-time, and actively participating at school events for myself and my children. My kids were no longer a stigmata and my inner voice that once told me, I will never be a single mom, now told me, Never say 'Never'!

I didn't have a high self-esteem, I did not think of myself as pretty or beautiful; even so, college is where I was given the opportunity to be a part of community fundraisers and was asked to participate in fashion shows. I started organizing and directing the shows. I also participated in collegiate speech tournaments and did well enough to win a few. I enjoyed it; it was fun, I found my voice!

Josephine with one daughter

I would use my voice to help bring child care to California's community colleges. Accessible education is important to me. When this movement began, a board member made a statement, "If men needed child care, this would have been done a long time ago."

I am still waiting for that department wing at the California community colleges, Child Care Services, to be named after me!

Josephine's Modeling Days

After one of the fashion show events, a woman from school asked me to go out to a nightclub with her and some of the girls. I was a young, "old lady," and I didn't want to party. All of my energy was directed towards school and being a good mom. Sometimes, I would forget my age, 26, and that it was healthy to go out and spend time with people my age, and socialize with my peers. I was serious about school. Even the fashion shows were strictly business. I had trust issues when it came to men and intimate relationships. I was not going to have every "Tom, Dick, and Harry" around my family. I had a team of other single moms; women who would help each other out with our kids and resources. We took turns cooking; I would make a big pot of food one week and then someone else would do it next.

Ms. Echols, you and I literally and figuratively walked down the same roads; we shared similar experiences of heartache and pain. At my age you had six children, I had four. At every fashion show, I felt like I was walking for you, Ms. Echols and Mrs. S, because I was doing things the two of you had never even dreamed of, things I never dreamt of, either. It just happened for me and I embraced it.

I no longer stuttered when I spoke and liked public speaking. While at a speech tournament, I met a woman who was fasting; we talked about God. She gave me a cassette tape, Amazing Grace, by Aretha Franklin. I listened to the album over and over; it gave me hope and I brought it home with me.

I always said to my kids, "Cleanliness is next to Godliness." The kids would wipe down the baseboards-they were always such a big help to me. While washing walls in the hallway of my home, my tears flowing, I felt that I was washing my sins away, as well. As people, on the outside, tried looking into my life, I would think, *You don't know the price of my alabaster box!* (Matthew 26:7)

I asked God if he intended for me to live alone in order to make me strong. If His plan was not for me to live alone forever, I asked that He would send me a good man. I had never been married and never thought I would; so, I did not ask for a husband but I did ask for a good man. I was protective over my kids and my heart; I would not allow just anyone in. There was a hurt and pain alive in my heart.

Josephine's Love Story

Ms. Echols, I found the freedom to be myself. It gave me power and that power was special.

My fashion club's modeling crew had wrapped up the fundraiser show for the new Mayor of Fairfield. I was, yet again, being asked to join them to celebrate. The night was still early; my boys were spending the night at a friend's house and my girls were at a slumber party, too. I didn't have a good excuse to not go.

One of the models, Chickie, asked, "Don't you like to dance?" While laughing, I said, "Yes, around my house!" She reminded me, "You don't have to stay late. You might have fun. You may even meet somebody!" I knew what she meant but I was not in a rush to be tied down to some man. I was at peace with my freedom, even if it meant that I was alone. I was ok with being by myself. Plus, I loved spending time with my kids.

I agreed to go dancing with my modeling crew at the Marina Lounge, that's where I met Thomas. We had just walked in and were heading to our table above the dance floor, just above the table where Thomas was sitting below with his group of friends. He looked up and we made eye contact. He pointed to his glass and mouthed the words, "Would you like a drink?" Through the music, I answered, "Lancer's white wine." We met and he asked me to dance. I loved dancing and took his offer.

Immediately he told me, "You're a friend of Chickie's. You know, I married the last friend she introduced me to. It did not turn out well for me. I have had bad luck with Chickie's friends." I looked at him and said, simply, "I'm not that kind of friend."

Thomas kept sending me drinks, which began to pile up at my table. I asked the waitress to stop bringing them. Thomas came to me, "You don't want my drinks?" I responded by asking, "Are you trying to get me drunk?" He said, "Maybe," with a little smile. I thanked him and expressed how flattered I was by his gesture, "But you could have just stopped after the first glass-I am not drinking much tonight. I just came out to dance and then I'm leaving."

He offered to take me to the dance floor. He was a pretty good dancer. A few songs played, we were still dancing. It seemed like the music was in slow-motion as we danced, checked each other out, and talked. Thomas was the perfect gentleman on the dance floor. He told me more about the story of Chickie's friend that he married.

Weeks passed, Chickie called me to ask permission for her to give Thomas my phone number. I said, "No but you can give me his." When I called him, he was taking a shower and took my number down by writing it on his mirror. He said he would call me right back. He did not call me back. A few days later, Chickie called, again. This time she was explaining how my number disappeared from his mirror when the steam evaporated, before he could write it down. He reached out to her to ask for my number, again.

Ms. Echols, with all the hurt and pain I carried in my heart, I felt I could not waste any time on any man. School, work, and my children consumed all of my time. I did not want to get hurt anymore. I didn't think my heart or mind could capacitate trauma again.

I allowed her to give Thomas my number. He called. We spoke over-the-phone for a while. He had a nice voice and asked if he could take me out sometime. Thomas told me of his schedule: he worked weekdays but on weekends he usually went out to the Marina Lounge. On Sundays, he attended church; then, he and his mother would have lunch and browse the flea market.

For our first date, he told me to choose, "It's up to you. Which would you like to do?"

Thomas was different from the other men I met-he was a gentleman. He took his time to listen to me. He gained my trust, after several phone conversations, and I gave him my address so he could pick me up on a Saturday evening.

My kids and I were doing our Saturday morning routine: cleaning. My family and I were preparing to go to the laundromat; we were packing three, huge garbage bags full of clothes and blankets. We were able to wash everything once a month. My son, Leo, had a drum kit in the garage. He was out there banging on the drums. He stopped and came to the bedroom, where I was loading linen, and said, "Mom, there's a man outside asking for you; he said his name is Thomas."

My heart dropped. My house was a mess, I was a mess! Why would he come so early in the day? I was not prepared to see him and I was not ready for him to meet my kids, yet. The reality was, my oldest son had already met him and he was waiting for me in the garage.

Ms. Echols, it turned out that Thomas had poor night vision and wanted to see where I lived before our date (this was before GPS on mobile phones).

I was happy to see him; it made me feel good internally. It had been a long time since I had smiled on the inside; I was good at smiling on the outside. You can never let them see you sweat!

Many nights were spent in my bedroom, the door closed, crying out to God. What I told The Lord was always just between me and Him. The door to my heart had been shut for a long time and as far as I was concerned, it would stay that way.

Leo and Thomas hit things off immediately. The drum kit was an icebreaker-they discussed music. Thomas asked how my day was going and I explained our housework, the cleaning, the trip we were about to do laundry. He asked for my permission to take Leo to a music store and offered to buy him a new pair of sticks and then meet us at the laundromat. I looked at my son to see his response to the offer and his face lit up with a smile. I had intended on buying my son new drum sticks but I never had the extra money. The drum kit was a gift from a friend and the drum sticks were badly worn. I allowed Leo to go but on the condition that he took his four year old brother, Mandela, with him.

Thomas and Leo loaded my station wagon with all of the laundry. My girls and I headed to the laundromat while the guys headed to the music store. Thomas was an exceptionally nice, caring person. He did not seem to mind that I had four children.

We would spend most of our time talking on the phone, getting to know each other. I often would read from the Book of Solomon, in The Bible, out loud to him until it was time for bed. The next night, we would pick up from where we left off, then discuss our thoughts and reflections about the scriptures. Usually, 30 minutes after I would begin reading, he would fall asleep. We both had a love for God and we both had pain from our pasts; our hearts hurt but weren't completely broken.

Our first official date was on a Sunday; Thomas took me to his church, Curry Temple AME, where he played the piano. His church was different from the ones I grew up in. (I never sang out of a hymnal book until then.) He had already been a member for 10 years. This man is too good to be true!

Thomas had a close relationship with his mother; he always talked about his father, who passed away two years before we met. He said he wished I could have met him. Around the holiday season, I was introduced to his mother, Ms. Aiko. She was a beautiful Japanese lady. She was a petite woman, her height at about 4'9", slightly round, with a very nice smile..

Thomas and his mother, Ms. Aiko

Before Thomas' mom, I had never met a Japanese person before. Ms. Aiko worked three jobs, not out of necessity but because she only knew to stay busy by working hard. That was how she survived WWII and life after.

One afternoon, I came to visit her. Everyone had to take their shoes off before entering her home. There was a dining room with a dinner table and big chairs but we all sat on the floor at a small table (That was also new to me). Thomas was not there; he had a music session to attend; Ms. Aiko and I had a chance to sit on the floor at the table together.

His mother asked me, "What do you want with my Thomas? What about the children's father?" I simply replied, "Ms. Aiko, Thomas makes me feel good, inside and out. He is so nice to me and my children. I have never met anyone like him. My children's father lives in another state and there will never be a problem with Thomas being in our lives. He makes me happy!"

I was all smiles-no shame in my game. His mother was a wise woman and Thomas was her only child. She had asked him about the pain in my eyes but he did not know why. He did not know much about my past because I never discussed it and he never asked. We were happy living in our moments together. We would go to church and go out dancing. We would get a bite to eat afterwards.

He was a gentleman and with his patience he gave me time before asking me to be his girlfriend; meaning, we would be exclusive to one another. Our intimacy had only led to long embraces and kisses. I hesitated out of fear that he would leave after he got what he wanted, like other men, then be on to the next one. I wanted more than sex-that was just letting a man on top to do his business, fall asleep, and wake up pregnant. I did not need any more children and I slept well by myself.

We were having a passionate moment of kissing, almost a year into our relationship, when Thomas asked to see my bedroom. I agreed, "You can see it." I made arrangements to have the kids out of the house for the night. I let him see my bedroom with a water bed, a study desk, a small TV, several books, and the walls completely covered with photographs of myself.

Ms. Echols, I knew I could please any man that I wanted. It only took about two minutes and then he would either be asleep or gone–but a man had never pleased me. A lifetime friend had thought it was so ironic that a woman with so much experience making babies did not know what a climax was. I confided in her, I didn't know I was supposed to feel pleasure.

The past experiences were all the same: I would lie there and wait for it to be over. There were times where I would close my eyes and make sounds, hoping that would make it end sooner. Receiving pleasure was new to me. My heart began to feel warm and comforted, the feeling of brokenness began to heal.

There was a day when I came home from school after picking up my kids. As I pulled into my driveway, I looked like the garage door was slightly opened. I scolded my oldest son, Leo, because it was his responsibility, "Didn't I tell you to make sure the garage door was locked?" I hoped there wasn't a burglary to steal what little we had. The garage door was lifted open and as I got to fully opening the door, much to my surprise, there was a washer and dryer in my garage. Thomas and Leo had planned it as a surprise for me. My very own washer and dryer, already installed to use!

Ms. Echols, my youngest, Azul, my baby girl, two years old, was sitting on the sofa with her feet on the coffee table. Thomas asked her nicely to take them off. Her response still makes me laugh, "You sound like a daddy. Do you want to be my daddy?" He just looked at her, smiled, and said, "That is up to your mom but I would love to help her take care of you and the rest of this wonderful family."

We did things together, like take the kids to the park, or to the boys' football games. He would help them with their homework.

My thoughts to myself would question the validity of his love. Is this man real? Why do I have a problem with how good he is? Is this all too good to be true? I had been living my life as pessimistic, like Eeyore from Winnie The Pooh, always dark clouds gathered over my head to block the sunshine. Pessimism made me believe that dark clouds lead to rain that would ruin and wash away any happiness that I had.

I received a call from Bakersfield. Mr. S' brother, the man with four kids and whose wife had helped me get Diamond back, had passed away. I was very sad. After I had given birth to Diamond, my family had told me that he was my biological father. That's why they kept me as part of the family, that's why Mr. S stepped up to raise me. I will always be grateful that Mr. and Mrs. S came into my life and chose me as their daughter, for taking care of me even though I was not theirs. Mrs. S gave me unconditional love and showed me that love covers a multitude of sins (1Peter 4:8).

Thomas was concerned about me and he did not understand that I didn't want to go back to my hometown, Bakersfield, even for a funeral service. He asked me if it was about money, and if so, he would help me get money to go .I needed to grieve the death in my own way and out of respect to his wife, I thought it was best that I did not go.

Suddenly, God spoke to my heart: If you want Thomas and want to share a lifelong bond together, you will have to heal your relationship with Mr. S. I thought to myself, How in the world can I do that? I searched The Word of God and found Matthew 6:12, which says, "And forgive us our trespasses, as we forgive those who transgress against us."

Epilogue

Ms. Echols, I will write to you again very soon! I cannot wait to tell you about the year I found all of your children! There is more information about my biological father I think even you are going to be surprised, and about my siblings on his side of my family. It has been the highest honor to relay messages of love from you! I have communicated with all of my brothers and sisters; the ones who knew you and the ones who knew nothing about you.

Like you, they grew to be loving people. *A good tree cannot bear bad fruit* (Matthew 7:17).

Ms. Echols, thank you for being a good tree. I cannot wait to share more Echols From the Grave and waves of my life with you. With science and technology we discovered facts about your great-grandfather, and how we are related to President Dwight D. Eisenhower.

With Love and Prayers,
Josephine

P.S.
1 Peter 4:8 *"And above all things, have reverent love for one another."*

About The Author

Alicia Ford is a wife, mother of seven (two sons and five daughters), a grandmother and a sister to 18 siblings. She lives in Southern California with her amazing husband of 30 years, Bobby Ford.

Before her writing career, Ford worked in the field of education as a yard duty and in-classroom aide. She worked for the Solano County Office of Education as a drug and alcohol prevention coordinator, as a grant writer to help youth stay off the streets by creating a safe place. In this position she was able to work alongside notable organizations such as: The Vallejo Omega Boys and Girls Club, MADD, domestic violence organizations, Habitat for Humanity, NAACP, BSU, PTA, and Solano College BSU.

Ford is an active member in her church's community. She is a member of her church's offices for The Church Of God In Christ (COGIC) including: the Usher's Board, Communion Board, and Prayer Board.

Ford is an activist and a Humanitarian; she volunteers her time, energy, and resources to do her part and make a difference in her community. Big or small works, it is all so that everyone can have an opportunity to sit at the table, so that every voice may be echoed with the intention of being heard.

Ford has been an active member for 20 years in her community church. She held several offices within her church, the Usher's Board, Communion Board, Prayer

Board, and the Mother's Board. Ford has been often called on to speak on women's day events, she is an activist and a humanitarian; she volunteers her time, energy, and resources to do her part and make a difference in her community. Big or small works, it is all so that everyone can have an opportunity to sit at the table so that every voice may be echoed with the intention of being heard.

When not planting seeds of inspiration in those around her, you can find Ford in her garden.

Catch the wave & Connect with Ford here:

Echolsaliciaford.com
Facebook.com/aliciaford
LInkedin.com/in/alicia-ford-echolsllc7
Instagram.com/echolsaliciaford
Send Emails to: *Echolsllc7@gmail.com*
Mail: 1730 18th Street #883 Bakersfield, CA 93301
Publisher: *Currybrotherspublishing.com/Echolsfrom-thegrave*

Got an idea for a book? Contact Curry Brothers Publishing, LLC. We are not satisfied until your publishing dreams come true. We specialize in all genres of books, especially religion, self-help, leadership, family history, poetry, and children's literature. There is an African Proverb that confirms, "When an elder dies, a library closes." Be careful who tells your family history. Our staff will navigate you through the entire publishing process, and we take pride in going the extra mile in meeting your publishing goals.

Improving the world one book

at a time!

Curry Brothers Publishing, LLC
PO Box 247
Haymarket, VA 20168
(719) 466-7518 & (615) 347-9124
Visit us at www.currybrotherspublishing.com